"What Goes Up ... *is an engaging tale of denial and its tragic aftermath. It depicts the inevitable downhill course of a man with bipolar disorder who denies his illness, and thus stops taking his lithium. And of his social worker wife, who also denies what is happening until it is too late. There is an obvious moral here for individuals with bipolar disorder and their families, and the book will be very useful for them.*"

—E. Fuller Torrey, MD has been called "The most famous psychiatrist in America" by the

Washington Post. He is a noted psychiatrist
specializing in manic-depres-
sion and author of *Surviving Manic Depression: A Manual on Bipolar Disorder for Patients, Families, and Providers.*

"*Powerful and informative. Judy Eron openly shares the sorts of devastation and tragedy that families all too often face when a loved one has manic-depressive illness.*"

—Lana Castle, author of *Bipolar Disorder Demystified: Mastering the Tightrope of Manic Depression*

"*First and foremost Judy Eron is a storyteller—and a very brave and honest one at that. The story she tells is poignant, revealing, and courageous. Judy's personal battle with her husband's bipolar illness has a tragic ending, but along the way we have a glimpse of true love, affection, and dedication. This story takes us up and takes us down. We experience the high of living life to the fullest as well as the lows of fear, confusion, and despair. It is a rollercoaster ride as seen through the heart and soul of a loving partner. We see first-hand both the stigma of mental illness from the outside and the denial of mental illness from the inside. This is a love song written by a survivor of suicide, at times sad, heart-breaking and frightening, yet at other times brimming with life, loving, and living. This story is a testament to the importance of treating bipolar illness from a biopsychosocial perspective. It is not just an endorsement of lithium but also a plea for collaboration between family and professionals. A must read for anyone who lives with mania, depression, or any of those psychological states in-between."*

—Morton M. Silverman, MD, psychiatrist and Editor-in-Chief of *Suicide & Life-Threatening Behavior*, American Association of Suicidology. He is also Senior Advisor to the Suicide Prevention Resource Center (SPRC).

WHAT GOES UP...

WHAT GOES UP...

Surviving the Manic Episode of a Loved One

JUDY ERON

BARRICADE
BOOKS

Fort Lee | New Jersey

Many of the names in this book have been changed in order to respect privacy.

Published by Barricade Books Inc.
185 Bridge Plaza North
Suite 308-A
Fort Lee, NJ 07024

www.barricadebooks.com

Library of Congress Cataloging-in-Publication Data

Eron, Judy.
    What goes up--surviving the manic episode of a loved one /
Judy Eron.
        p. cm.
    Includes bibliographic references.
    ISBN 1-56980-285-8
1. Eron, Judy. 2. Eron, Jim--Mental health. 3. Manic depressive illness--Popular works. 4. Caregivers--United States--Biography. 5. Manic depressive persons--United States--Biography. 6. Manic depressive persons--United States--Family relationships. I. Title.

RC516.E76 2005
362.196'895'0092--dc22
[B]   2005041063

First Printing
Manufactured in Canada

DEDICATION

This book is dedicated to Jim's family who share with me the memory of this wonderful man who should still be here with us.

CONTENTS

FOREWORD
Xavier Amador, Ph.D.

This book is a must read for anyone who has a loved one with serious mental illness who says "I am not sick, I don't need help!" Judy learned many hard lessons while dealing with her husband Jim's bipolar disorder. Her goal in writing this book is to turn her family's tragedy into something positive and useful to others. She has done this and so much more. I am grateful to her for having the courage to write this book. Once you have read *What Goes Up*, you will be too.

This book does not review the new research that has proven to be helpful to many family members and therapists trying to convince someone to accept treatment. Most of that research was published shortly after Jim's death. Such a review was never the author's goal. What this book does is bring an all too common story (about 6 million American families are dealing with a mentally ill loved one who does not believe he is sick) to life in a way that educates and heals.

I could not help but experience Jim's anger, paranoia, and ultimately the alienation he suffered because he could not understand that he was sick and in need of treatment. Jim was a psychologist who had once come to the conclusion that he needed to be on medication for the rest of his life. How could a psychologist and informed patient suddenly decide he had it all wrong, ignore the warning signs that were blatantly obvious to all around him and persist in the belief that there was nothing wrong with him? Some might be tempted to say it was a flaw in his character or that it was caused by an unhealthy desire to hold onto the manic high. Without being didactic, the author makes it clear this severe lack of insight was a symptom of the brain disorder, not an irresponsible choice to be high.

Jim's unawareness of the illness drove him from the woman who loved him most, it drove him from his family and further into the delusional world the bipolar illness had created. Judy's steady empathy for her husband and her ability to separate the illness from the man while preserving her own sanity is remarkable and something to be emulated.

By her example, she teaches readers about the common pitfalls such as denial about a loved one's illness. Denial in Jim's family is portrayed for what it is: a desperate attempt to not alienate the mentally ill loved one by expressing directly your worry, an ultimately doomed attempt to keep him near and safe. Like so many families I have known, Jim's family was held hostage by the illness, at first fearing direct confrontation because of the rage and "disappearing act" that would follow. Judy explains, by example, how this happens and what it takes to free yourself from the prison created by anosognosia (a symptom of bipolar disorder and schizophrenia that renders the person unaware that he or she is ill).

Among the hard won lessons she learned, Judy discovered the value of backing off the goal of convincing a loved one to get help. Her goal shifted from getting Jim into treatment (which only alienated him and made him run further) to gaining his trust. To that end, she also stumbled on the power of apology. A heartfelt apology for not agreeing with the mentally ill person's view of the world (even delusion), for not having been better equipped to make things better, for any part played that can genuinely be apologized for, immediately deflates and diffuses the anger and paranoia and provides an opening. But before uncovering such valuable lessons, Judy and her family made all the common mistakes (the same mistakes I made early on when my brother became mentally ill) like "holding their ground" and unyielding confrontation about the question of Jim's mental illness.

Judy lays out the common pitfalls encountered by family members in this situation. The powerlessness, self-doubt, loss of self-esteem and depression that she felt are common. I have no doubt that her candid description of her experience will be healing to others. It is one thing to hear the platitude "you will be no good to anyone if you're not taking care of yourself" and it is quite another to see someone struggle through the guilt and fear to come to that conclusion for herself.

Once I started, I could not put this book down. It is ultimately a love story. It is about love persevering in the worst of all possible conditions. I have treated many couples and have found that mental illness is one of the most common causes of divorce.. Usually, it is an untreated mood disorder. Untreated mental illness transforms loving, responsible and caring partners into seemingly apathetic, irresponsible and even cruel strangers.

Although the illness cost Jim his life and exacted a terrible toll on Judy, *What Goes Up* is ultimately a hopeful book because of the many battles won by this couple. Judy and Jim were deeply in love and the illness very nearly convinced them both that they were not. That is the ultimate triumph of their story. The survival of their love for one another and the power of that love to heal.

* * *

Xavier Amador, Ph.D. is a clinical psychologist in New York City and adjunct professor at Teachers, College, Columbia University. He is the author of *I Am Not Sick, I Don't Need Help! Helping the Seriously Mentally Ill Accept Treatment* as well as *Insight and Psychosis* and *When Someone You Love is Depressed: How to Help Without Losing Yourself.* The former Director of Research at the National Alliance for the Mentally Ill (NAMI), he is now on their Board of Directors.

PREFACE

This manuscript, begun during the year Jim was manic, sat in pieces on my shelf for four years as I worked at putting my life back in order after Jim's suicide. The events were still too present, I was too much in their grip. The story was not yet a story to tell: It was still too much the reality I was living.

Over time, however, despite thinking I never could or would, I made a new life. I moved back to the house Jim and I had built on the secluded mountain desert outside Big Bend National Park in southwest Texas, the house in which Jim killed himself. I recommitted myself to writing and fell in love with Roger, an anthropologist. We married, and I was back in life, having found the ground again.

I felt strong and sure and able to resume writing this book. Rereading what I had written thus far was not easy, but it was not crushing, either, as it would have been earlier.

As I began my efforts to reorganize and reconstruct what I had written, I decided to consult certain materials that earlier had been too raw and painful to examine. With this much time elapsed, I felt sure that I could be objective and use the material to help present this story, this intention of mine to write something that might be helpful for someone in my shoes.

Innocently, I sorted through Jim's writings from his year off lithium. It was a good sign and a relief that his handwriting no longer brought me to tears. Then I listened to some tapes that each of us had recorded that year. One was a tape Jim made while intensely manic, as he drove away from our life in August 1996. Another was recorded by me, off by myself during my first visit back to our home in Texas that December, in which I describe a horrible incident that had just happened between us.

Listening first to the tape of me, I was shocked and disturbed to hear myself rationalizing Jim's behaviors and holding myself responsible. Describing the incident to myself, I was agreeing with Jim's position that I was wrong to look at him with a diagnosis, wrong to think that he was manic, and I was agreeing that I had characterized him unfairly to our friends and family. Even as I described an ugly incident that involved Jim screaming malicious accusations at me, insisting I follow impossible rules, punching the plastic windows of our Jeep, I spoke as if he had been making sense and that it was I who needed to shape up and go faster to keep pace with him.

As I listened to this tape, I was alarmed to hear myself sounding so weak and confused, more like a battered spouse identifying and agreeing with her abuser. I felt sad hearing myself having lost my own center, having lost the belief in my own perceptions.

However, when I listened to Jim's recording, I understood. Just hearing his words and inflections on the tape, I felt myself caught up in his charge again, beginning to question myself again, to fill with the same doubts I had back then. Jim was four years dead and yet the strength of his conviction that nothing was wrong with him, the might with which he hurled his accusations at me, the skill with which he attacked my vulnerabilities, which he knew intimately—these all served as darts piercing my present reality, darts that lodged in my heart and presence of mind. I could feel my clarity draining from me just as it had four years before.

Although quite painful, it was actually helpful that I revisited Jim's perceptions and my responses—hearing his wild and preposterous ideas, hearing myself so compliant. It reaffirmed my belief in the need for this book and my wish to be writing something helpful for those who might find themselves in a similar position, to help them stay sane and on track, and to avoid the self-esteem nosedive I took.

I want this for you. You will need all your strength and courage to deal with your loved one during the manic episode, and most certainly after. Because, may I remind you: *What goes up must come down.*

—Judy Eron
April 2005

ACKNOWLEDGMENTS

I would like to acknowledge the following people, for various reasons:

Sadie Rossen who gave me a home during my homeless year of Jim's illness.

My aunt, Bub, who became a widow two weeks before I did and still had love to give me.

My cousin, Ellen Diamond, a careful and demanding editor in the early drafts of this book and a significant support throughout.

Dr. Stanley Bodner for the BowWow Ballet.

Patty Hall for pushing me towards finding a home for this book.

Greg Armbruster for knowing there was a book in this story.

Acknowledgments

Marge Wall for more than once helping me pick up pieces in the aftermath.

Mary Makenna, there through it all.

My friends who are therapists, who gave endlessly: Linda Stere, Beverly Burch, Linda O'Brien, Karen Schwartz, Michele Bograd.

Dr. Rob Jamieson and Dr. Hal Goldberg for their generosity.

Dr. Xavier Amador, whose work I wish I had found sooner.

Rabbi Yoel Kahn, Carl Smith, and Mark Enterline.

Geoffrey Morgan, Paul Jones, Dean Young, Pam Check, Carolyn Schwartz, Lori Ellison, Jane and Jerry Brewster.

Pablo Garzon and Rob Jackson for the musical joys of The Bad Year in Nashville.

Howard Maloney, Michael Zande, Susan Hoffman, Donna DiNovelli, and Jane Harris, for traveling down the road of loss with me.

Sue Dixon, Holly, and my other first readers for their invaluable feedback on my manuscript.

The Samaritans of New York City for providing Safe Place.

My brother and sister-in-law, Larry Eron and Donna Cheng.

My nieces and nephews, Ethan, Lucy, Amanda, and Chips, for compassion beyond their years.

My cousins, Alan and Hiroko, Mark and Anne, Alan and Janis, and Mutzie, for their concern.

Acknowledgments

Roger Boren, for tolerating my voyages back in time to a former life.

I sent a query letter to Carole Stuart of Barricade Books. She called me immediately to ask me to send my manuscript, saying that my letter had landed on her desk at the same time that she was dealing with the manic episode of a friend of hers. This sort of coincidence has tailed me ever since Jim became ill, implying that manic-depressive illness seems to touch most people's lives in one way or another. I thank Carole and Lyle Stuart, Jennifer Itskevich, and Jeff Nordstedt for taking this story personally and then taking a chance on me, and Sandy Stuart for her supportive editing.

Lastly, I am forever indebted to the many people whose lives have been touched, strained, altered by manic-depressive illness who have repeatedly appeared out of nowhere, but who have requested to retain their privacy. I will assure myself that you know who you are, with hopes that our contact touched you as it did me. And I trust that you will find satisfaction in knowing that all the help you gave me, whether it was during the living or the writing of these chapters, I am now passing along in the form of this book. Thank you.

DSM IV: *Manic-Depression Diagnostic Criteria*

Diagnostic criteria:
   Current or past *manic episode*
   May have a history of *major depressive episode*

Manic episode:
   A distinct period of elevated, expansive, or irritable mood
      lasting more than one week.
   Marked impairment in occupational functioning or in usual
      activities or relationships with others; may necessitate
      hospitalization to prevent harm to self or others; or there
      are psychotic features.
   Three or more of the following:
   • inflated self-esteem or grandiosity
   • decreased need for sleep
   • more talkative than usual or pressure to keep talking
   • flight of ideas or racing thoughts
   • distractibility (i.e. attention too easily drawn to unimpor-
      tant or irrelevant external stimuli)
   • increase in goal-directed activity or agitation
   • excess involvement in pleasurable activities that have a
      high potential for painful consequences (e.g., engaging in
      unrestrained buying sprees, sexual indiscretions, or fool-
      ish business investments)

Major depression:
   Five or more of the following symptoms for at least two
   weeks:
   • depressed mood most of the day
   • markedly diminished interest or pleasure in activities
   • significant weight loss, weight gain, or change in appetite
   • insomnia or hypersomnia
   • psychomotor agitation or retardation
   • fatigue or loss of energy
   • feelings of worthlessness or guilt
   • diminished ability to think or concentrate
   • recurrent thoughts of death or suicidal ideation

INTRODUCTION

It is a strange set of circumstances when a wife wakes up every morning wishing her husband would get severely depressed or arrested.

It is a strange set of circumstances when a wife wakes up every morning hoping that her husband has an automobile accident that puts him in the hospital for an extended period of time.

It is a strange set of circumstances when a wife wakes up every morning praying that her husband will be caught running naked in the streets.

I lived in this strange set of circumstances for more than a year, wishing, hoping, praying for these very things. Any of them might have meant the possibility of my husband returning to me.

My husband Jim had manic-depressive illness. He was

diagnosed in 1983 following a psychotic depression. He was prescribed lithium, which he took for the next thirteen years. Nine of those years were with me, and they were wonderful years.

However, in June 1996, Jim suddenly stopped taking lithium. Within weeks, he was in a full-blown manic episode, which stretched on for more than a year until late September 1997, far longer than anyone imagined it could last.

When he finally came down from his mania, he came down fast and hard, sliding swiftly into a severe depression. On October 11, 1997, Jim put a shotgun in his mouth and killed himself.

This could be a book about suicide, about surviving in the aftermath of this devastating way to lose a loved one. There is certainly much to say on the subject, and several good books are available for "suicide survivors" as they call us, a rather twisted nomenclature. But suicide is only part of manic-depressive illness in the way that leg amputations, dialysis, and death are part of diabetes—a possible outcome, although not the inevitable course of the illness. One should neither be blind to the possibility nor be an alarmist about it, only vigilant and prepared.

Jim's suicide, although devastating and unimaginable, was only one scene in a larger drama that surrounded it. That drama is the subject of this book: the mania of manic-depression.

A person who is manic presents his views emphatically and is extremely persuasive in his perspective that it is everyone else, not he, who is acting differently and who is responsible for the chaos. His mind is sharp, and his perceptions are heightened. As Jerrold S. Maxmen and Nicholas G. Ward describe in their text, *Essential Psychopathology and Its Treatment*, "They play the 'manic game,' in which they are constantly testing everybody's limits; they manipulate others' self-esteem, perceive and exploit people's vulnerabilities, and project responsibility."

The people who love that person can get heaved off balance. They need resources for ballast. During the year that Jim was manic, I searched for people to talk with and books to read to assist me in staying grounded. I wanted to know how best to deal with him, what to expect, how to hang in, yet not be damaged. Although there was a lot to read on depression, there was surprisingly little to read about loving someone who is in the midst of a manic episode, especially if the person cannot be hospitalized.

This book is intended for those who love someone who is in the manic phase of manic-depressive illness. I hope that what I present will serve as a counterbalance to the persuasive voice of the manic person. My wish is to help normalize and dilute the feelings of impotence, guilt, confusion, and self-blame that can only weaken a caring person and make that person more susceptible to the impaired reasoning and countless accusations of the person who is manic.

This is not a how-to book in the usual sense, for I did not know how. Nor is it a how-not-to book. Manic-depression is far too individual an illness for that. I simply want to present my experience, which I hope will help you to continue to trust your own perceptions and stay strong. You will need your strength.

While the manic person is flying high, so full, so convincing, so strong, it does not seem possible that he or she will ever crash. This is especially true if it goes on and on as it did with Jim. However, eventually the mania will run itself out, and what almost always follows is a deep and dark depression. This is when the potential for suicide increases dramatically and is also when you will need a great reserve of strength.

I did not have this reserve. No one gave me this specific counsel, that how you deal with the person when he is manic sets the stage and influences how you will deal with him when he becomes depressed. What weakened me and slaughtered my ability to be of much help when Jim eventually, but so quickly, plunged into depression was how confused and ungrounded I had become during the year that he was manic. The problem over and over again that year was my inability to remain clear and certain that Jim was mentally ill. Manic-depression is a cycling illness, and Jim was not cycling. Almost everything I read stated that an untreated manic episode usually lasts three to six months. As the months wore on, I lost the belief that Jim would ever crash.

In addition, Jim was incredibly forceful in his argument that he was not mentally ill, an argument supported by all the interesting projects in which he was involved. Over time, I fell more and more into an acceptance of his reality and into a state of doubt about my own perceptions.

I know you love your person, so I would never suggest that you not have hope. Rather, it is my wish to help you balance hope with reality. Hope is a good thing. Love is a good thing. But with someone who is manic, you will need a special kind of love. I hope that my experience will give you a basis of comparison so that you will stay alert and not get shaken.

Jim and I were a loving and functional couple. Although we both naively believed that the power of our love would keep Jim healthy, we had talked at length about his illness, had made plans of what to do if he were to become ill again. In addition, we were mental health professionals with years of experience. We thought we were equipped to handle such a crisis.

What neither of us knew was the full power of his mania once it owned him. We did not know that it could convince him that I was his enemy. We did not know that all plans we made for dealing with his illness were useless once he was looking at these plans through unmedicated eyes.

Nor did we know how fractured I would become by his changes. Jim's mania made him a stranger to me, and I had almost no ability to deal with this stranger. Usually a strong person, I was paralyzed and intimidated by his ferocity, arrogance, and certainty. All my skills as a therapist went down the tubes.

This book is about learning to live with making choices from a list of only unappealing ones. There is no "Column B" on this menu. In a way, there is little "right" that a caring person can do; however, there are plenty of "wrongs" to try to avoid.

Everyone who knew and loved Jim, everyone I consulted about manic-depression including those with manic-depressive illness, their family members, many psychiatrists, and other mental health experts—*everyone* believed Jim would crash much sooner than he did. Something would stop him the way it had before, the way it usually stops a person who is manic. No one expected his mania to go on for as long as it did, with him able to live unmedicated and able to not come down or get into trouble for more than a year. No one.

As it turned out, although much later than anticipated, in the end, everyone was right:

Indeed, what goes up must come down.

It's Sobering

It's sobering how little I really know you.
It's sobering to think what could go wrong.
I don't know how we've gone so fast.
Nor do I know why we would not last.
But it's sobering, at the very least.

And it's serious what's going on between us.
Yes, it's serious how much we're starting to care.
We can hope the future will be
Just as bright as these first few weeks.
But it's sobering, at the very least.

It's just so wonderful how one day we had nothing,
And then the next we had each other.
It's just a marvelous trick, so precise and slick,
Something that Nature picked, designed to entertain us.

But it's sobering to think how little I know you.
It's sobering to think what could go wrong.
So many risks, as there always are,
When you get close with so many scars.
And it's sobering, at the very least.

Song by Judy Eron
Written March 17, 1987

WHAT GOES UP...

Part One: June 7, 1996 - September 8, 1997

1

MADE IN A LABORATORY

I used to say that Jim was made in a laboratory for me, created specifically according to my needs and wants in a mate. He was romantic, sexual, sensual, fun, introspective, responsible, adventurous. When we first started seeing each other, Jim told me that he was looking for a partner, someone with whom to face life, to share responsibilities and tasks. I told him I took that as a given in a mate. What I wanted was someone who would sustain romance the way I desired to and knew I could. In the years that followed, we continually marveled that we had both gotten what we were seeking. As Jim put it in one of his many cards and notes to me over the years: "To rediscover with you my capacity to love and lust and long, as unexpected and strong as it is, has been wonderful and unnerving, not to mention this desire welling up in me to trust this bonding with you I feel."

Jim and I were a good couple, a functional couple, a creative couple. We were loyal and devoted to one another, yet also highly independent in our own pursuits. Supportive of one another's endeavors, we trusted each other to want the best for each of us separately and particularly for us as a couple.

I had never had that before. I called Jim "my big grown-up man." The other men I had partnered with had been less able to express and deal with feelings. Although I had been married in my twenties to my college boyfriend, the marriage had deteriorated until he finally left to be with another woman, which did much damage to my view of my desirability as a woman. Two subsequent relationships were somewhat healing for me, each about four years long. However, neither was destined for longevity.

Jim and I were different. Jim was the first man I had ever been with who took the lead in building our relationship, suggesting ways for us to grow together. We had wonderful creative approaches for working out our disagreements and were always able to resolve fights without blaming. Each of us claimed a share of the responsibility for any tensions. Whichever one of us apologized first could always count on the other one apologizing, too. Jim put it this way in one of his notes: "I love how consistently you come to patch the hurts that sometimes slip from us." Our motto was: If one of us loses, we both lose.

We were proud of ourselves in many, many ways.

Jim and I met in 1987 at a mutual friend's Super Bowl party. I was thirty-eight, recently out of a relationship, and Jim at forty was only just beginning to date after his divorce two years prior. He had been married for eighteen years and had two sons. Each of us was in private practice, I as a social worker, Jim as a psychologist testing children. Coincidentally, we were living just around the corner from each other, there in Nashville, Tennessee.

I was not initially attracted to Jim. At the time, I did not find bald men appealing and was not excited when he asked me out. But as we spent time together, he turned out to be fun, interesting, and remarkably insightful. He had a sharp wit and a willingness to speak very personally.

We did not even hold hands or kiss for the first month, just talked and talked. Gradually, we began to be physical, and about two months into the relationship, we spent our first night together.

That first night was sweet and tender, and we were both amazed at how easy it was to be together. There seemed to be no obstacles.

Then, sometime in the middle of that night, while we were just lying looking into one another's eyes, Jim said, "Judy, I have to tell you something. Something that's not easy to talk about."

I felt my heart stop as he went on. "I'm bipolar—manic-depressive. I take lithium. I've been taking it for four years." He said this straightforwardly, with no apology in his voice.

Equally straightforwardly, I responded, my head beside his on the pillow, "That's sobering."

This was the first in a series of disclosures that Jim made to me over the next seven months, disclosures about his mental illness, substance-abuse history, and hospitalizations. He was always truthful and candid, and by the time we were married in October 1987, I knew all about his many losses and sorrows, his depressions, his manic episode, the medicine, the family history of manic-depression. He never tried to soft-pedal or lighten this dark picture of his multiple humiliations and the damage to his first marriage and his two sons. He wanted me to know fully what I was getting into so that my choosing to be with him would be a deliberated, informed choice.

Jim's own willingness to admit to the enormity of his situation allowed me to accept him, to accept all the mind-boggling pieces of him. I was already in love with him; the fact of his illness did not diminish this for me. He was committed to taking his lithium and was grateful for its stabilizing effects. He was also in psychotherapy and attended a lithium group at the Veterans Administration Hospital, where he received his medication.

Jim was also committed to not using marijuana, which had gotten him into trouble professionally. His position was that marijuana was like a mistress who could interfere with our relationship. He also vowed that he would attend AA if his two-beers-a-day drinking policy showed signs of getting out of control.

It seemed certain that Jim was dedicated to me and to us and was not willing to jeopardize either. As he wrote, "Truly, yours is a serenity that lets me touch softer places in myself than I've known."

Shamefacedly, I have to admit that I tended to glamorize Jim's mental illness. It was something so out of my ordinary life experience to be involved with someone who was manic-depressive, someone who had actually wandered the streets in a psychotic state and was now a wonderful, fully functioning person. Because Jim was so okay, it seemed safe to think of his past as exciting and exotic. His disclosures were scary and perplexing, but also intriguing.

Despite having worked in the mental health field for fourteen years, I was not very informed about manic-depressive illness. The only people I had met whom I knew to be manic-depressive were on the psychiatric units of hospitals where I had worked, and they were quite disturbed. I have since learned that many wonderful, creative, highly successful people have manic-depression, but I did not know that before Jim's crisis.

Because Jim was so "normal" in every way, such a terrific person, his disclosure did not cause huge alarms to go off in me. Not that it was neutral either. I was worried about this new development. Still, only half-joking, I put it to my best friend, Mary. "Well, what do you think? Am I letting myself in for another relationship with a damaged man?" But it was impossible to imagine Jim as anything but the remarkable man he obviously was.

As for Jim, he was head over heels. Since his divorce, he had been alone and celibate and was now ready to plunge ahead. And I was delighted at my fortune in finding a man so able to love, so at ease expressing his feelings.

It was as blissful as it sounds.

Jim was honest. I was naive. We were both ignorant. To put it mildly, we underestimated what his illness meant to us—the destruction it could cause and the havoc it could wreak, havoc that would eventually be our demise.

We overestimated the power of love in the face of mania.

We married while on a camping trip to Big Bend National Park in Texas. In his clever and romantic way, Jim had called ahead and secretly made arrangements for the wedding. He proposed in the middle of the desert, and we were married a few days later by the judge in a nearby town. The next day, we climbed the highest peak in Big Bend and exchanged rings, reciting vows of "why I want to marry you" that we had prepared. It was all quite wonderful and quite Jim.

During our nine good years together, we kept our romance alive with fabulous trips, simple kindnesses, cards, and gifts. One of the best things we did for our relationship was what we called "appreciations." Every Sunday, we would reserve a special time to tell each other the things we appreciated about our own lives and about each other. These might include things like a chance we had to help someone, or something someone else did for us, or just about the beauty of the lilies growing in our yard. Always included were acknowledgments of one another for the joys of being together. These "appreciations" were great nourishment for our relationship.

We each said that it was our first time of feeling that we really knew how to love another person, to love so that the other person felt loved. To be successful at love is a precious thing, and we felt we were there.

From the start, Jim led us to try things in order to

become closer, to learn more about each other, and about how we dealt with things together. Even before we married, Jim suggested we experiment with intertwining our moneys and our work more. Toward this end, we opened a joint bank account, although we each kept our own money, too. Over time, we felt more comfortable sharing most of our mutual life expenses.

We also merged our professional lives by starting a couples therapy practice. In particular, we worked with many people dealing with HIV and AIDS and volunteered as group leaders with our local AIDS organization. We were both very committed to service work, and watching each other work gave us a chance to admire each other's skills and vulnerabilities, which in turn strengthened us as a couple and enhanced our love.

Yet another way we found to interweave ourselves was in our religions. Rather than giving us a cause for difference, Jim's Catholicism and my Judaism gave us opportunities to celebrate together. Especially at Easter/Passover time, we would get together with family and friends to tell the stories and perform the rituals of both holidays.

Jim and I wanted to have a baby. He had two sons, but I had never had children, and we wanted to be parents together. However, despite our own efforts and some modern-day medical-miracle attempts, we never did become pregnant. This was a big sorrow for us, but coping with it brought us even closer. After a few years of trying, we decided to turn the disappointment into a new dream, and we began the plan for what we called our "Getaway."

Ever since our first trip to Big Bend National Park when we had gotten married, we had returned twice a year, falling more and more in love with the area. We decided to look for land there and found a huge ranch that was subdivided. We bought forty acres with a small shack built of straw bales. Our "casita," as we called it, became the beginning of our Getaway plan. One upside of not having a baby was a certain financial freedom, and we conscientiously saved money in order to move permanently to the casita and expand it into a home. Our Getaway would be a chance to live a very different life, to explore other interests, other ways to be of service, and a way to intertwine ourselves more.

Jim and I were a good team and in just a few years managed to save enough to accomplish our move. We purchased a truck and travel trailer to live in while we built the house. We bought an old Jeep for the desert and budgeted enough for the house building. Since the desert was far too hot for summers, we also found a small lot on the coast of Washington State where we could live in our travel trailer during the summers.

Another preparation for our Getaway related to the large amounts of time we would suddenly have to ourselves. We knew that building our house would consume us for a while. We loved reading aloud to one another, playing recorder duets, and hiking. I was already a singer/songwriter and intended to develop myself further as a writer with the leisure of our Getaway.

Jim, however, had no hobbies of his own. In anticipation of our Getaway, in his disciplined planful way, Jim took photography courses, and in fact by the time of our Getaway, he had already had his first show.

The final piece of our preparations for Getaway was to establish some sort of volunteer service work. The American Red Cross was the perfect answer, and after completing training, we became volunteers on national disasters that took us all around the United States and even to some tropical islands.

There is one special detail I want to mention. While we were still working, Jim, in his uniquely romantic and creative way, gave me an unusual birthday gift—two twelve-inch tall glass canisters, one filled with small black glass stones, the other with a single black glass stone in it. He explained that this was to be our symbolic countdown to our Getaway. Each day until we left, we dropped one stone from the full canister into the emptier canister. The full one gradually emptied as the empty one filled, until it was time to go.

This was so Jim. It exemplifies an aspect of him I loved dearly—that he could acknowledge the importance of small concrete things and see their connection to our process of joining. I had always been the sort of person who loved to send cards and observe special occasions, as I wanted to be deeply connected to those I loved. I had longed for a partner who could be attached in this way, who wanted what I wanted about love and romance. And here he was, my husband.

Our Getaway was an elaborate plan, a methodical plan, a united plan. In May 1993, we closed our practices and moved from Nashville to the Big Bend in Texas.

However, somehow in our Getaway plans, we had managed to completely avoid the subject of a mental-health support system for Jim's manic-depression. By that time, he had been stable on lithium for ten years. We must have felt there was nothing to worry about.

From May 1993 to June 1996, Jim and I lived an unusual lifestyle that was totally dependent on our being together. It was designed as a dream for two.

Living in our travel trailer in the remote mountain desert of southwest Texas, we spent those three years building our home with our own hands. Neither of us knew the first thing about building, and yet there we were pouring a foundation, putting up walls, installing windows and doors. We laid tiles, put up ceilings, wired the whole house ourselves. Knowing nothing to begin with, we designed and installed an elaborate solar-power system, a rain catchment system for our water supply, and completed our beautiful home looking out at the Chisos Mountains of Big Bend National Park. It was a good example of one plus one equals far more than two.

Although we worked hard, we still hiked, played our recorders, and helped at disasters with the Red Cross. In the summers, as planned, we pulled our travel trailer to our lot in Washington State where we fished and wrote, took pictures and read aloud to one another.

We were on our own. Jim described it as an experiment in being out in the world relying only on one another. It was an extraordinary life, fun and full of joy. I had everything I had ever wanted.

During this time, Jim and I did two exercises in which we each wrote what we would change if we knew we only had six months to live and what we would do if someone gave us ten million dollars. Amazingly, neither of us came up with much; we were already living life as we wanted. We had the desert, our writing, photography, music, and opportunities to help others.

Most of all, we had each other.

2

JIM'S HISTORY

Jim was born in Milwaukee, Wisconsin, on November 1, 1946, the second of five children. His family was Catholic, and Jim attended parochial schools, then the University of Dayton, a Catholic institution. He was an altar boy in church and basically a good boy and an obedient son, although he had one summer of excessive drinking when he was a sophomore in high school.

It was a shock to the family when Jim married at age twenty-one and had his first son while still in college. Already a responsible young man, Jim now found himself loaded with more responsibility. He was hooked into early adulthood, prematurely giving up youthful adventure and fun—and this in the sixties, the decade of "freedom" when his peers were out experimenting with different lifestyles. Despite having a wife and child, Jim was afraid he might be called up and sent to Vietnam after receiving a low draft lottery number. He joined ROTC and then the army, both of which further constricted his life. Jim entered the army full time in 1973, after receiving his Ph.D. in psychology from the University of Iowa.

In those early years, Jim performed his roles very well; he was responsible and dutiful. In our talks, he did not mention any periods of excessive moodiness during that time, although by his own description, he was overly authoritative with his children, especially his older son. In all, he was a devoted and loyal father and husband.

However, as his work brought him into contact with a broader range of people and experiences, cracks developed in that responsible self. As Jim explained it to me, when he began to smoke marijuana, his end as a family man began.

From 1976 to 1979, Jim did postdoctoral training then worked at Walter Reed Hospital in Washington, D.C. There he met a psychiatrist in residency with whom he would smoke marijuana and extemporize on the nature of life and various other philosophical and psychological topics that were new to him. It was a grand and liberating time for Jim that also, for better or worse, provided an escape.

According to Jim, his wife understandably felt very threatened by these changes. Her husband was reaching outside the family for support, friendship, and fun. He said that he felt her holding on more tightly, and as a natural consequence, he pulled away more.

Interestingly enough, however, he told me that he

did not roam sexually. Jim was a still a good Catholic boy.

Jim came to realize later that his first clinical depression occurred in 1980 shortly after his transfer to Germany, where he was appointed clinical director of a drug and alcohol unit in an army hospital. Because he was self-medicating with marijuana, Jim did not recognize his depression at that time. He was eventually caught with marijuana and was sent to a rehab clinic in California for six weeks. Amazingly and unfortunately, he told me that even there, his depression was not diagnosed.

When Jim returned to Germany, he was not discharged from the army, but was let go from the directorship position and sent back to the United States to be stationed at Fort Campbell, Kentucky. Soon after, he sank into a serious depression that mushroomed into psychosis. Reality slipped away from him, and he disappeared from both his family and the army.

For seven weeks, Jim lived unrecognized and undiscovered on the streets of Nashville, just an hour from his home. His AWOL status made front-page news. Eventually picked up by the police, he was hospitalized at Fort Gordon in Georgia. There he was diagnosed with manic-depressive illness, and he began to take lithium in January 1983.

Lithium controlled Jim's depressions. In fact, except for a few days here and there, Jim was never clinically depressed again until he discontinued lithium in 1996, flew off into mania, and then crashed into his final suicidal depression.

These days it is common knowledge that manic-depressive illness is genetic. Jim's family was no exception. His mother was diagnosed after her retirement, much later than is usual, and took lithium the rest of her life. Her own mother had killed herself many years before, probably also bipolar. Jim's older brother was diagnosed in his twenties and has taken lithium since then. Jim's father was alcoholic and when he stopped drinking late in life, suffered from depression. Jim's next younger brother suffers from depressions and diagnoses himself "cyclothymic with hypomanic episodes," a closely related, but much less severe form of mania, and the youngest brother struggled against a serious drug and alcohol problem in his younger years. Only Jim's sister, the last born, has remained free of both mental illness and addiction problems.

After being diagnosed in 1983, Jim received a medical discharge from the army with a 30-percent disability for manic-depressive illness. Needing to reconstruct his life, he moved his wife and sons to Nashville, where he worked with both a mental health center and the Catholic diocese.

As I said, lithium worked wonders for the depression side of Jim's manic-depressive illness. But in 1985, he had what is known as a "breakthrough mania," which means that even though he was taking his normal daily dosage of lithium, his brain chemistry altered for unknown reasons, and his regular dosage was temporarily inadequate.

This manic episode lasted several months, initially just energizing him, but eventually running Jim out of control. It culminated at the mental health center where he worked. He was reportedly talking wildly, which frightened the other workers. The police were called, and Jim was taken to the state hospital. His blood was drawn, and surprisingly, he was found to have the appropriate lithium level. Jim's wife persuaded the hospital to release him to her care.

That night, Jim left his marriage. He simply could not conform to that mold anymore, particularly in his manic state.

The psychology board charged Jim with inappropriate professional behavior and suspended his psychology license for two years. He was able to find employment with a small mental health center testing children and lived with the director and his family for several months. He entered therapy with a seasoned female therapist in Nashville, took his lithium religiously, and participated in a group at the V.A. Hospital that consisted of male veterans diagnosed with manic-depressive illness. The group was led by a pharmacist with expertise in lithium, and the emphasis was clearly on helping the members adjust to living with the drug.

Jim's sons had been exposed to some bad situations at a young age due to Jim's illness, and it was several months before Jim was able to face his shame and see them again. But eventually he rented his own apartment, and his sons stayed with him every other weekend. Jim continued to do psychological testing of children, built a solid reputation, and was much sought after professionally. He joined a men's discussion group for friendship, but otherwise spent his time alone. He remained celibate and had only just begun dating when we met two years after his divorce.

Despite all the chaos that his illness caused, Jim did

not let shame eat him. He was open with me about his illness and his messes, as he was with his friends and both our families. It was not a taboo subject. I admired him for this. As with so much about Jim, the less positive things about him were intertwined with so much good.

3

WARNING SIGNS NOT HEEDED

Elizabeth Hardwick, the writer married to poet Robert Lowell who suffered with manic-depressive illness, wrote:

> No one has the slightest idea of what I've been through with him. In four and a half years, he had four collapses including this one—three manic, one depression . . . I knew the possibility of this when I married him, and I have always felt that the joy of his "normal" periods, the lovely time we had, all I've learned from him, the immeasurable things I've derived from our marriage made up for the bad periods. I consider it all a gain of the most precious kind.

Even in retrospect, I do not wish that I had run from Jim or denied the relationship. What I do wish is that I had known enough about manic-depression to have insisted that we have deeper and more personal therapeutic assistance. Our minimal relationship with the V.A. was not adequate for the seriousness of Jim's mental illness nor was Jim's psychotherapist a specialist in manic-depression. All along, Jim should have had a private psychiatrist who had specific expertise in manic-depressive illness, and I should have been part of that process. In addition, we should have sought a group for couples dealing with manic-depressive illness.

There were warning signs early in our relationship, some of which should have had me loudly insisting that we go to a specialist in manic-depression. The first event occurred in June 1987, about four months into our relationship.

Jim had arranged for me to meet his family. He had set up a gathering at Tim's Ford State Park in Tennessee in July. It was to be my first time meeting everyone—his parents, his sister, Cass, and his brothers, William and Roy. Jim's two sons were to be there, along with William's fiancée and Cass's three small children.

I put a lot of energy into making it a success, swimming, playing volleyball, taking long walks, and talking with various family members, including Jim's older son, and Roy, Jim's next younger brother. I played with Cass's children, helped cook the meals, and did my best to adjust to all the people. Being a family person myself, I enjoyed Jim's family. It was a fun week.

Soon after that week, however, Jim and I were on a

walk, talking about the time with his family. Suddenly, out of nowhere, he confronted me harshly with the accusation that I had acted seductively towards his father and his brother, Roy. He said I had been too friendly and had been duped by them both, taken in by their seductive ways. He accused me of having a flirtation with them, of being foolishly naive, and said that I had made a fool of him.

Jim was severe and furious, full of cynical, sharp, rough, stern condemnations. I was startled and couldn't believe that he was actually serious. His warm, loving, beautiful face was contorted, impenetrable. For those minutes, he seemed to hate me, holding me guilty of betraying him.

I felt like the police had me spread-eagled up against the wall and I had to talk my way out of a false arrest or conviction. It was horrible. I could not believe that Jim could really be thinking that I was attracted to his father or brother or that I cared anything about either of them other than as extensions of him. And how could he think I would ever betray him like that? I asked him. He wasn't understanding the depth of my love, my connection to him, nor my loyalty to him. He was sure I was not understanding how his father and brother were at work seducing me. We talked and talked. At last, Jim softened and began to accept that I was just trying to be nice to his family for his sake and that I loved only him.

When I look back, it's clear now that Jim was way too intense about this, maybe even temporarily delusional. I do wonder why I did not take this more seriously, did not put it through a sieve of mental health, did not see it as a danger sign. Because it was. This same delusion repeated itself ten years later, during Jim's mania, vis-a-vis Roy. Jim revisited the Tim's Ford incident, reviving his accusations and suspicions, giving Roy and me "free rein to pursue any relationship" we wanted, which was absurd.

Jim was moody and very sensitive to both real and imagined slights by me, even the smallest ones. Instead of expressing his anger directly, he would withdraw, and we would have the following dialogue:

Judy: What's wrong, Jim?
Jim: Nothing.
Judy: You're acting cold, being really quiet. What's wrong?
Jim: Nothing.

He would continue to be withdrawn for a few hours until I would finally get angry at his unresponsiveness. Once I became angry, he would admit his own anger and hurt, usually about something I had no idea about.

These were uncomfortable episodes, but we were always able to talk about them later. Each of us would apologize for our part in the discomfort. I did not like it that Jim was so ultrasensitive in this way. However, it was Jim's ultrasensitivity in other ways that I loved so much and that made being in a relationship with him so extraordinary. Furthermore, our "it takes two to tango" view of our relationship strengthened us as a couple. We trusted each other enough to believe that we would always come out of these fights in a better place, having learned something important and valuable.

As I write of warning signs unheeded, a paradox of

sorts emerges: The very events that should have and could have served as warning signs were instead times that usually brought us closer together.

I can recall three episodes in our good years when it was clear to me that Jim's withdrawal was not just moodiness. Two of these occurred when he was taking lithium; the third happened during the three weeks between his stopping lithium and the full onslaught of his manic period.

Jim referred to these as "psychotic depressions." Although each was brief, lasting only a few days, they were alarming and disturbing while they were happening. Each time I wondered whether and how the episode would end.

The first time was during our first summer as a couple. It was triggered by an ugly situation that arose out of nowhere, shocking us both, pointing up the difference in our life experiences.

We were enjoying a wonderful, active, sensual sex life, when Jim suddenly developed strange symptoms—sores on his genitals, a white substance in his mouth. Not having a clue what this was, we went to a clinic where they immediately tested him for HIV, thinking the white substance was candida, an early symptom of HIV. It was not. They were stymied, so we went to a dermatologist, who diagnosed this as Stevens-Johnson syndrome, an allergic response to a virus, the virus being herpes.

Herpes. A crashing, crushing blow. Where would Jim, with his limited sexual experience, have gotten herpes, except from me? It did not matter to him that I had never (and have never) had any symptoms of herpes.

Riding home from the dermatologist's office, Jim was quiet and became quieter and quieter, until finally when we arrived back at his apartment, he lay mute and unresponsive in bed. Jim's previous withdrawals had a transparent purpose of punishing me. This was different. I had never seen someone "take to his bed" and disappear inside himself, almost catatonic.

It was horrible. I had no idea what was happening and no idea what to do about it. Amazingly, it did not occur to me to contact Jim's therapist, although in retrospect that would have been a wise thing to do. We would have alerted her to the fact that his depression was still lurking.

It lasted about five days. Somehow Jim managed to get out of bed every day to go to work. But he was totally uncommunicative with me, and I grew anxious that maybe our relationship would end.

I don't remember how we made the transition back to normalcy. Probably, after several days of trying to coddle him, I got angry. When we were able to talk about it, Jim described his anger at me and his despair at having a second incurable illness, and of all things, a sexually contracted illness that could feed heavily into his jealousy. Although he never again had any symptoms, the herpes became fodder for his venomous accusations ten years later.

This awful experience hurt me and shook Jim's belief that his depression was under control. It was a big surprise and disappointment to him that depression could still swallow him. I remember only vague bits about how we managed to assimilate this lapse into our growing and deepening relationship. I cannot reconstruct why neither of us took this as the proverbial wake-up call to find a consultant, to learn more about manic-depressive illness. Perhaps being therapists ourselves skewed us in some way. More likely, it was plain old denial. Dangerous denial.

The incident, however, did have one good outcome, one way which Jim and I used to prepare ourselves. Jim constructed a list of guidelines for me to follow if he were ever to get that depressed again. Here is the list:

1. Ask him to "surface" for a few moments so we might have a sane conversation. "I don't like this, Jim. I want you back. But do what you have to do. Is there anything you'd like to say, for me to know?"

2. Refer to the depression as "it," not "you." "Isn't *it* terrible when these things happen? Doesn't *it* feel like a wet blanket covering you up?"

3. Say, don't ask, "I'm going to be here. If you don't want me to be here, you'll have to tell me, because otherwise I'm choosing to be here."

4. Give full permission for being depressed. In addition, however, tell him to fight it. Stir his anger towards being combative against the depression. "You're not responsible for getting where you are, but you are responsible for doing something about it."

5. Remember that anger is part of depression. He is pissed off at his situation, angry at being in a body and mind that are so sluggish, like a quadriplegic person may feel at his body.

6. Use sarcasm. "Good morning, Jim, look what a bright wonderful day this is."

7. Do low-energy, low-social intercourse activities, like walking together or going to the movies together.

8. Remember that a depressed person wants strongly both to be alone and to be together. He cannot be reciprocal, so he is embarrassed and self-conscious for the nondepressed person, feeling a certain shame that he's making the other person feel awkward.

9. The silence of depression is not voluntary. The only thing he feels he has to say is "I feel awful."

10. I should get him to medicine, and I should go along with him.

I should have been carrying this list with me every day of our relationship. Instead, it was tucked into a file somewhere. When Jim became manic and I became so ungrounded, I don't think I remembered that we had made such a list. I am ashamed and dumbstruck that I never consulted it. If I had had this list in front of me in October 1997, I wonder whether I would have known to just go be with Jim in his final depression.

It is also true that by the time Jim slid into depression, I was worn down. I probably would not have taken the risk of trying to do the things on this list anyway for fear that Jim would reject me again. The point of this book is to help others to not get worn down as I was.

There may have been other reasons I didn't carry the list with me. The first instruction, for example, always struck me as peculiar. If Jim could exert enough self-control to "surface" in order to deal with me, then couldn't he exert the self-control to be a functioning, responsible adult? If not, why not?

Clearly, I was not getting it about the lack of control a depressed person feels. In *Darkness Visible*, his book about his own depression, William Styron poignantly describes being in the clutches of depression and ". . . the basic inability of healthy people to imagine a form of torment so alien to everyday experience." Jim always distinguished between what he called "Big D-Depression" and general depression. I have never experienced "Big D-Depression." The only times I have felt what I would call "depressed" have been in response to a depressing event: relationship breakups, death of my mother, reactions considered "normal."

Despite my being a mental health practitioner much of my adult life, I still did not fully understand then, nor do I understand even now, the helplessness of being Big D-Depressed. If I did, perhaps I would have applauded Jim's saying he would surface to deal with me.

The second of these episodes occurred in 1993 when we went to Washington State for the first summer of our Getaway. We had overtaxed our bodies packing for our move, and Jim's back was bothering him. He had major back surgery just two years before, so this greatly worried him.

A few days after arriving at our land by the ocean in Washington, I said something that upset Jim, something about wanting to shop around for an electrician. As before, Jim got quieter and quieter until he was in bed and not getting up or responding to me at all.

I was frightened and upset. Here we were at the very start of what we had planned so carefully and so looked forward to. We had deliberately designed this life to intertwine us more so we could be together all the time, and Jim was disappearing, abandoning me, deserting our "us-ness."

When Jim's first mute depression had occurred in Nashville, at least I had been near my friends, my work, and in familiar surroundings. Up in Washington State, I might as well have been on a deserted island. I knew no one there.

My confidence in "us" was shaken by this. That Jim "entitled" himself to retreat, to leave me so abruptly and unilaterally, scared and confused me. I felt he was distinctly out of bounds and that mental illness did not absolve him. Although I knew this was depression, I was furious with him.

In the thick of this episode, I wrote in my journal: "I awoke early and could barely hear his breathing in his efforts to 'not be.' No snoring. No life. I touched him a little. No reaction."

Then a bit later: "I was determined to talk to him. He talked, just a little. Miserable about his back. 'Laying low' is what he said. I suppose he has to use very little space in order not to bump up against the walls of his despair. I told him plans to meet the electrician, etc. He seemed vague and perplexed and a little contrary. (Anger might actually help, be preferable.) I told him I need him, said kind of lightly that he's all I've got. He said he wasn't planning on staying in bed. Then he said that he's going for a walk."

I continued: "It is sad to think that I can't cause alteration in him about this, that our relationship isn't what he can hold on to in his misery, and let me be there, too."

Then days later I wrote: "It is a week since Jim was 'sick' (our word now for it). Things have been fine, he is very loving. But it hovers, how he can withdraw at what seems to be his own discretion. And he said it was not Big D-Depression, which pissed me off that maybe it was more of his own choosing. Weird to choose catatonia as a personal option."

As I said, this episode only lasted a couple of days. Once again, I really cannot say what ended it. I do remember talking about the initial disagreement that had been the trigger and clarifying what had happened, whatever it was. But no amount of processing could make it okay how Jim did this retreating. What mature adult has the right to shut his spouse out so entirely?

But somehow once again I integrated this episode into our relationship. We did not seek out additional counsel about manic-depressive illness, did not consider a medication change for Jim. Nor did we seek any relationship counseling. I'm just not sure what we were thinking, and it is deeply troubling to think back on. I also don't remember consulting Jim's instructions from the similar episode six years earlier. Had I misplaced them? Forgotten them? Our carelessness is more evidence of us being too casual about his manic-depressive illness.

It is hard to believe how Jim and I, savvy mental health professionals, could ignore the significance of these seriously strange episodes instead of taking proper steps to get more help. As I write this, I feel stupid, ashamed, and utterly aghast that we failed to heed the significant warning signs I have described. These incidents reflected the power of Jim's mental illness and the powerlessness I could feel in the face of it. Separately and together, we rationalized it out of fear and denial, neither one of us wanting to see the river of Jim's mental illness rushing underneath our exciting, wonderful, loving life together.

4

SUDDENLY, THE LAST SUMMER

The demise of our relationship, and ultimately of Jim, began June 7, 1996, the day we left Texas for our fourth summer in Washington State. We were three hours into our trip, only three hours from our Texas home, when Jim said, "I forgot my lithium."

We had just celebrated the completion of our house on the desert. It had been an intense three-year project, our only breaks being the trips with the Red Cross as disaster volunteers and our summers in Washington. Our house was beautiful, and we had built it together. Jim's parents had come down from Milwaukee, and neighbors joined us for a party. We were proud of ourselves, proud of our home, and ready to rest.

If we had known then what I know now, if we could have read this very book that I am writing, we would have turned around and headed home for Jim's lithium.

We should have known to do that. But on June 7, 1996, we did not know the gamble we were taking.

It's not as though we ignored the issue. Jim was disturbed enough to call the V.A. Hospital in Big Spring, Texas, from which he received his supply of lithium each month in the mail. He was told that he could either stop at another V.A. or they could send his lithium up to Washington so it would be there when we arrived. Jim investigated the availability and location of V.A. hospitals on our route and found that there were none close by. We decided to wait and have them mail the lithium to Washington.

Jim was letting me in on the decision, and I was not worried. Jim was handling it and seemed sincerely invested in being responsible. The prospect of two weeks off lithium did not disturb me, nor, I thought, him. (He told me later that he was immediately conscious of being off lithium, feeling scared, risky, and excited, too.)

So much to say here. We were just ignorant, massively ignorant about the possible consequences of being off lithium so suddenly. We did not know an essential fact, that abruptly stopping lithium can trigger a manic episode. Jim had been taking lithium for thirteen years. In those thirteen years, Jim had rarely even missed a dose, let alone been off it for days at a time. It seems simple common sense that a person would not, should not, stop it abruptly—it is a mood stabilizer. In retrospect, our decision seems immensely foolish.

What I learned later is that lithium has a half-life of twenty-four hours. This means that half of it is out of a person's system in just one day's time. Lithium is completely out of the blood in five to seven days. Not knowing this, I think our logic went that since Jim had taken lithium for thirteen years, surely he had a reserve stored up inside him.

Most importantly, this was Jim, my responsible, mature, savvy partner. I trusted him and respected his opinions and judgment. I did not get it that without lithium, with his natural body chemistry, Jim would not have a choice. And although I had seen him depressed, I had never seen him manic. He had described his 1985 manic episode, had told me many painful details of his pressured and uncontrolled behavior. But without having seen it, I could not possibly begin to imagine its true horror. And of course, I never thought that would happen to us.

Another part of the equation was that we were dealing with a V.A. that did not know Jim. At the Nashville V.A. Hospital, Jim had his monthly lithium group, led by a pharmacist who knew Jim and his manic-depression well. But in Texas, Jim received his medication in the mail from the V.A. in Big Spring, where he was only seen in person every six months for lab work, by a different doctor each time. No one there really knew Jim.

Hence, when Jim called to report his forgotten lithium, he spoke with someone who failed to mention that he was playing with fire. Probably it was a receptionist who never checked with a psychiatrist. Whoever it was did not know manic-depressive illness and the danger of being off medication, especially suddenly, cold turkey.

Had we had a private psychiatrist, had the person who took the call known Jim and remembered his history or been someone who knew enough about manic-depressive illness, that person would surely have told us what we were dealing with. That person could easily have called in a prescription to any pharmacy, and we would have picked up lithium that day. That person would have known this was an emergency. That person might have saved Jim's life.

Instead, blissfully ignorant, Jim and I drove on toward Washington. We drove leisurely, not even hurrying to get there to the waiting lithium. We had a wonderful time camping at our favorite spots in the red rock country of southern Utah. Things seemed fine to me, with only some minor tensions.

Later, Jim said that he had stayed very aware of not taking lithium. Although it seemed to me we were having a great time, Jim said later that he was "already feeling too good."

We arrived at our land in Washington on Friday afternoon, June 21. As expected, Jim's lithium was waiting with our other mail.

However, over the next few days, I noticed that Jim was not taking it. I could easily observe this since he normally left his next dose out on the bathroom counter. When I asked him about it, he said that he didn't want to talk about it right then, but would talk about it soon. That satisfied me. Jim often had his own schedule for talking about important things, and I trusted him to return to the subject.

I was not preoccupied with this as I was still peacefully ignorant about the implications of this action. A few days later, when Jim said, "I'm ready to talk to you now about lithium," I was glad. But I really did not expect him to say what he did.

"I've decided not to take it."

Or maybe he said, "I've decided to *try* not taking it."
I'm not certain whether the word "try" was in his dec-
laration and so can't be sure if he was viewing this as an
experiment or a new lifestyle. But my guess would be
the latter.

I could feel myself a little nervous and concerned,
but not freaked. Once again, ignorance was bliss.

He went on. "I intend to be responsible about this,
Judy. I'm going to get a consultant, someone to have in
our lives as an ally for either or both of us to talk with
as I do this. I don't take it lightly."

That sounded reasonable to me. Although I felt
nervous about it, it was a nervousness born of the unfamiliar, not from some dread or expectation, certainly
not born of any prediction or premonition. Just that Jim
had been taking lithium since before I met him; his
twice-daily medication was part of the fabric of our life
together. Neither of us knew how that fabric could or
would unravel without it.

To repeat, my/our ignorance was astonishing.

But it is also true that in my innocent, well-meaning
heart of hearts, I felt that Jim had a right to try life without medication. After thirteen years, it did not seem
unreasonable. In addition, by then he had been off lithium for two-and-a-half weeks and seemed no different. I
was used to respecting Jim's assessment of his illness
and state of mental health and had no reason yet to stop
trusting that ability.

I learned many things later, too late. I have already
mentioned one of these, but it deserves repeating. I
learned that the abrupt stopping of lithium can trigger

a manic episode. In addition, a lot later, I learned that Jim was smoking marijuana for the first time in our nine years of marriage. "I saw God," he later said to his brother, Roy. He told Roy he had purchased it eight months earlier, but presumably had not smoked any of it until our summer trip.

The significance of this is twofold. Not only was Jim smoking marijuana again, something that had gotten him into deep trouble before and which is known to aggravate manic-depressive illness, but he had also been carrying around a secret for the better part of a year.

People always ask, "Why did he stop taking lithium?" In truth, I never got the chance to know the answer because Jim never got well enough for us to have a balanced discussion about this. With time and a much greater understanding of the illness, I have come to believe that it was a combination of at least three things.

1. It is part of manic-depressive illness to want to be off medication. As with many people taking medication to treat a chronic condition, there is the wish to be off the medicine. If the person is doing well, he can easily think that medication is no longer necessary. Also, there may be unpleasant side effects. (Lithium's side effects can include diarrhea, a hand tremor, dry mouth, and kidney problems.) Manic-depression adds to this the lingering allure of the high of mania. Goodwin and Jamison state in their textbook, *Manic-Depressive Illness*: "The first reported instance of lithium non-compliance in a manic-depressive patient was the first patient treat-

ed with the drug." This is especially true because "cessation of lithium is accompanied often by relatively immediate positive experiences."

2. Jim had been on lithium for thirteen years. The year before we left Nashville, he had discussed with the pharmacist who led his lithium group the damage that lithium might be causing his kidneys. At that time, Jim was exploring the possibility of stopping medication. However, weighing the pros and cons, he decided to stay on the drug. But it is likely that this idea was still bubbling within him.

3. I feel sure that Jim honestly forgot to bring his lithium, but I think that this was unconsciously motivated. I learned as the days went by, as we talked, while we still could talk, that Jim had been wondering for a while, even before our trip began, whether lithium might be working on his thinking and subduing his concentration, his creativity, and spontaneity. Only a month earlier, we had read aloud a book Jim's father had given us, *An Unquiet Mind* by Kay Jamison, Ph.D. Dr. Jamison is coauthor of *Manic-Depressive Illness*, a widely respected clinical book. *An Unquiet Mind* is her personal story of her own manic-depressive illness. She describes how she felt that for some time she was on too high a dose of lithium and that it clouded her thinking and suppressed her creativity. This sounds quite similar to Jim's thinking. With each passing day Jim was off lithium, this line of thought became more and more seductive to him, as he felt himself walking a high wire and liking first the notion and then the effects.

Dr. Jamison also describes in no uncertain terms how lithium has saved her life, what a shambles her life became when she was off lithium. However, despite all her precautionary advisements, she actually writes of her mania with a certain lust and longing.

> The countless hypomanias, and mania itself, all have brought into my life a different level of sensing and feeling and thinking . . . I have been aware of finding new corners in my mind and heart. Some of those corners were incredible and beautiful and took my breath away and made me feel as though I could die right then and the images would sustain me.

From Jim's underlining in this book, it seems clear that this influenced him, reminded him of the energy and wonderment of mania. Simply put, I believe that it is significant that we read Kay Jamison's book in May and Jim discontinued lithium in June.

In any case, we agreed for him to proceed without lithium. Was it just coincidental or was it actually taking the lid off things that almost as soon as Jim announced his intention, he became different. Jim stopped lithium on June 7, 1996. We arrived at our summer spot on June 21. He told me on June 25 that he wasn't going back on lithium. June 28 is my first vivid memory of Jim's behavior being different.

It was a Friday, and we had driven to the town of Astoria where we did most of our shopping. It was a beautiful drive hugging the Columbia River, passing people fishing for sturgeon, crossing the long bridge to Oregon, watching as seagulls traced a path along the guardrails. In town, we stopped at the photographic supply store. That was when I first noticed Jim being different with other people, and it was the first occasion, but one of many to come, of my feeling embarrassed to be with him.

The owner, Chuck, was waiting on a customer. I was looking for a phone book. Jim went to Chuck and interrupted, without any "excuse me" or other politeness.

"Hey, Chuck, this is my wife, Judy. Judy, this is Chuck. Judy needs a phone book, Chuck. Do you have one?"

Chuck looked bewildered and then miffed that he and his customer were put in this awkward situation by Jim's interruption. I mumbled a "glad to meet you" or something, but felt embarrassed, as if Chuck might have thought I had made Jim interrupt him just to introduce me.

Being used to respecting the gentle and observant ways Jim ordinarily dealt with people, I was stunned by this. Jim, on the other hand, was oblivious.

Other signs emerged of Jim becoming higher. He was a man who, although very productive, could also sit down and relax, read a magazine, nap, read the paper. However, now he was restless, on the go, spending a lot of time driving around, unable to settle down.

There were longer and longer stretches when Jim was awake in the night, sometimes not coming to bed at all. I would awaken at 3 A.M. to find him at the table, full of energy. Before, Jim and I had always gone to bed together. We would snuggle, with one of us reading aloud to the other. It was sweet, important time together. Now he had no patience for such reading; this closeness was gone.

Jim realized, more than I did, that he could be in trouble if he did not get sleep. He knew this and told me, tears accompanying his fear. From his manic episode eleven years earlier, he knew that not sleeping was both a symptom of and a trigger for a manic episode. But he was not frightened or upset enough to reverse his decision to be off lithium.

Jim initially had stated that he wanted to be responsible about his choice to not take lithium. There were two parts to this. The first was a set of instructions that I was to follow. The second was his intention to find a consultant for us.

The set of instructions went like this:

1. Never call the police unless I think he will hurt me or someone else violently.

2. Never try to contain him myself.

3. If his behavior becomes intolerable to me, then a) I should call his brother, Roy, or his best friend, Paul, and/or b) I should leave and go to my cousin, Frances, in New York City.

4. Treat him now as I had treated my psychotherapy clients; that is, no judging. Make him feel safe that I am not seeing him as crazy.

5. Clue him in if I think he is being weird with people.

6. If I am uncomfortable with him in a social scene, get us out of it by saying, "Jim, sorry, I have a stomachache and need to go."

7. Do any of this calmly, softly, nonhysterically.

8. Maybe help him/us get to the desert. "Jim, let's go back to Texas."

Jim had me write these in my journal. They were well-intentioned, but ridiculously insufficient once he was in the throes of his mania.

The second part of Jim's intention to be responsible about not taking lithium was his search for a consultant for us. Coincidentally, in the small community in which we were living in Washington, a naturopathic physician had just opened a practice. She was young, perhaps twenty-six or so, serious, and expensive. Jim decided to consult her for help sleeping.

Maybe naturopathy was not at fault, but rather this young woman's lack of experience. Whichever, it turned out to be a huge mistake to use her as our only consultant.

Jim asked me to come to his first meeting with her in which she asked him many questions. He cried more easily in those initial days of his becoming manic, and he wept through much of the hour-and-a-half appointment. He kept garnishing me with compliments about my devotion to him, his trust in me.

Jim talked to the naturopath about his past. He described his life with his first wife and his sorrow for the pain he had caused her and his sons with his manic-depressive illness.

At the time of this appointment, Jim was not denying his diagnosis of manic-depression. He just wanted to treat it without lithium. However, he had already lost some insight, judgment, and perspective and was to lose a lot more quite quickly. He was already fairly blind to his behavior changes.

The naturopath resolved to consult with someone

she had heard speak on treating bipolar disorder with naturopathic remedies. Meanwhile, she gave Jim various Chinese herbs to help him sleep. Jim's sleep improved immediately, but it was improvement from one or two hours to at most four hours, broken up throughout the night. He determined that he should not go to sleep with me, but rather should stay up, take the herbs late in the night, and get the sleep all at once. So our cuddling was quite abbreviated compared to the previous nine years, and I missed it.

With Jim sleeping so little, almost anytime that I awoke, he would be at the table (we were living in the tiny environment of our travel trailer) writing figures, compiling data, sorting his photographs and negatives. This was in his nature anyway, to make lists and charts—really good ones. But now I could see that it was excessive and pressured.

Jim went to the naturopath several more times. Initially he encouraged me to call her if I wanted, that he needed nothing kept private from me. However, as he rapidly became more manic, his paranoia increased, and he soon forbade me to call her. I never did, and then one day, she called to ask me to come to a session with Jim without clearing this first with him. This breach of their relationship caused him to stop seeing her. By then it didn't really matter; Jim was convinced that he needed no treatment.

Jim's first appointment with the naturopath was on July 3. At the Fourth of July parade, I got another early glimpse of Jim being strange and different. He was taking a huge number of photographs and being more than a little pushy about "getting his shots." Indeed, he actually stopped the progress of some of the paraders several times for a photo, getting in front of people, blocking others' views. And finally, in the jerkiness and pressure of his movements, he dropped his camera, cracking the telephoto lens.

It seemed that overnight Jim became more social, interested in visiting with anyone he met. No longer did we take simple walks together. He was engaging us with more people, and I was repeatedly embarrassed by him.

It grieves me to say that. The bedrock of my love for Jim was my respect for him. I liked how gentle and supportive he was when he dealt with people. Now he was acting brash and inappropriately familiar, more like the self-centered people we usually avoided.

One distastefully memorable time was with a couple. Jim took the bus into town from our trailer and got into conversation with the driver. From this came Jim's decision that we should get together to play bridge, although the man's wife did not know how to play nor did she want to play. Jim kept calling them, pushing and pushing until finally we met with them. An unpleasant time ensued at their home during which Jim was taking liberties being sarcastic and jibing when he hardly knew these people. It took a lot of energy to contain myself; I so wanted to apologize for his behavior. I could not wait to get out of there, which we finally did. Mercifully, we never saw those people again.

Another series of situations concerned a nearby farm that Jim wanted to photograph, especially the old farm equipment, rusting, decrepit, and quite beautiful. He was told that the people were very private, so when he got permission from the elderly woman living there, he considered it "a major coup." It was disturbing to hear him recount this, bragging about his prowess and people skills, his manipulative courting ability. It was becoming more and more difficult to trust his appraisal of situations.

There was more to this. "I could tell you some things, Judy, but you might find them disturbing. Do you want to hear?"

I hesitated. "I don't know, Jim. Let's try."

"Well, there are these three dogs that the woman has, and one is part blue heeler. I was out in the field with them, and it became clear that we had telepathy going on, those dogs and I. We were sending messages back and forth. Sounds crazy, huh?"

What was I to answer? Jim and I had always left some room in our thinking and view of the world for paranormal or "fringy" occurrences, so I didn't want to negate his idea that he was in communication with the dogs. On the other hand, for him to feel and say such a thing was creepy given all of the other changes in his judgment and behavior.

There were physical changes, too. For nine years, Jim's lunch had consisted of a soda, pretzels, and a candy bar. Suddenly, it was a soda and cheese and crackers. For breakfast, he had only ever wanted toast. Now he craved an egg. I'd always been a big water drinker and used to encourage him to drink more water, especially when we were on the desert, but plain water did not excite him. Now he wanted water, a lot of water. He needed windows open, needed more air.

And what was to become a major focus of our tensions, he started smoking cigarettes again after a three-year abstinence.

Looking back now, I know that my harping on Jim's smoking was more a reaction to the other changes that were happening so fast, but I focused my fear and frustration on his smoking. It was also a reaction to the way I found out that he was smoking. One day he asked me to get his glasses out of his pack. When I unzipped it, there were the cigarettes. Having been married to a man years earlier who had a secret sexual life, I was sensitive to secretive behavior. Jim, knowing this, apologized, adding, "There are no women, Judy."

But later, that would change, too.

5

THE SUMMER ENDS

With each day that passed, things got more and more out of control, and our separation grew. Jim's irritability increased. He became discontent with the ocean community where we lived in our travel trailer and decided that he no longer wanted to own land there. He wanted us to sell immediately and go elsewhere.

He started looking at land on his own. Involvement in any business venture was very out of character as Jim had always hated wheeling and dealing. But there he was calling Realtors, making appointments, keeping lists on clipboards, driving far and wide. He already had little energy and time for us, and now there was even less. Our time together became almost nonexistent.

By this time, we had been in Washington for about five weeks. Each day, Jim lost more perspective on his behavior and unusual thinking until finally he felt himself to be misdiagnosed and wanted to sue the company that makes lithium, charging that they had sedated him unnecessarily.

I tried to stay in rhythm with him, tried to keep him in my mind and heart as my beloved husband. But it was difficult and lonely being with him. He was a stranger. His body looked like him, but I recognized him less and less. I felt more and more lost, abandoned, and angry.

In his book, *Electroboy, A Memoir Of Mania*, Andy Behrman writes his "to do" list of January 6, 1991.

1. Bleach bathtub, toilet, and sink
2. Make Holocaust documentary
3. Start tofu/tuna diet
4. Work out five days/week
5. Buy new scale
6. Confirm $35,000 wire transfer from Art Collection House
7. Open Munich bank account
8. Open escrow account for rent
9. Mail $20,000 to American Express
10. Bring $2,700 to Dr. Kleinman
11. Submit claims to Blue Cross/Blue Shield
12. Go to Metpath lab for lithium level
13. Pick up lithium and Prozac
14. Buy more Kiehl's Extra Strength Styling Gel
15. Get Lara's psychiatrist's phone #
16. Get Pamela's astrologist's phone #

17. Tanning salon
18. Visit Auschwitz
19. South Beach or Bahamas?
20. Book trip with Dad to Galapagos
21. Make reservations at Chanterelle
22. Write novel and screenplay
23. Read 7 *Habits of Highly Effective People*
24. Pick up Liquid-Plumr
25. Buy a dog

Jim's list might have looked similar. "Criteria for Manic Episode" in the *Diagnostic and Statistical Manual (DSM IV)* describes Jim perfectly at that point:

- A distinct period of elevated, expansive or irritable mood lasting more than one week.

- Marked impairment in occupational functioning or in usual activities or relationships with others, or to necessitate hospitalization to prevent harm to self or others, or there are psychotic features.

Three or more of the following [Jim had *all* of the following]:

- inflated self-esteem or grandiosity
- decreased need for sleep
- more talkative than usual or pressure to keep talking
- flight of ideas or racing thoughts
- distractibility (i.e. attention too easily drawn to unimportant or irrelevant external stimuli)
- increase in goal-directed activity or agitation

- excess involvement in pleasurable activities that have a high potential for painful consequences (e.g., engaging in unrestrained buying sprees, sexual indiscretions, or foolish business investments)

Beginning around June 28, off lithium for three weeks, Jim was visibly spiraling into mania, and soon after, his mind was peppered with delusions. By mid-August, he was accusing me of absurd things such as thinking he was anti-Semitic. Jim was deep in the midst of a manic episode and continuing to feel that nothing was wrong with him.

In *Run, Run, Run: The Lives of Abbie Hoffman*, Abbie's brother, Jack Hoffman, describes Abbie's behavior off lithium:

> Abbie had begun to ignore his medication needs completely. I was scared. I saw Abbie in front of me, but I didn't recognize him. There was a wildness in his eyes, a furious and unappeasable rage. His speech was rapid and slurred. I couldn't see any recognition of me in his look. I felt I wouldn't have been able to stop him from hurting himself or me if he'd wanted to. And it seemed like he wanted to. So I just helped him move out; there was nothing else I felt I could do. I was so frightened and confused, it did not even occur to me to seek psychiatric care for Abbie.

This aptly describes Jim on Friday, August 23, two-and-a-half months off lithium, when the last vestiges of the Jim I had known totally disappeared.

As we were preparing to leave Washington for our

return trip to Texas, Jim's behavior changed even more radically. We had planned to park our truck and travel trailer at Travis Air Force Base in California, then fly to Hawaii to help my brother and his family move into the house they had just built. However, Jim was even more irritable and fast paced than he had been up to then, and I think he could see in my face that I thought he was acting bizarrely.

His projections and paranoia became more pronounced. (Projection is characteristic of a person who is manic, the act of ascribing to someone else one's own attitudes or thoughts.) He was saying things like, "Judy, you need to be on medication. You obviously cannot control yourself. You are cycling even more than me." He began referring to how everyone else thought he was okay and how I should go to Hawaii by myself, adding that then he might have to find another woman. "It's your anxiety and fears, Judy. They're destroying us."

I said, "Jim, we need a third party." This launched him into a lecture. "I have many third parties, and everyone but you, Judy, thinks I'm fine." He became frantic, finally announcing that he was leaving, that we had to be apart for the night, and he would meet me at a nearby restaurant the next morning at eight. "And you better come alone—no cops, no women friends, no neighbors." His eyes looked very wild and scared.

Back at the end of June when he was still clear in his thinking, Jim had advised me in his set of instructions that if he began to behave in ways I could not deal with, I should call Roy or his best friend, Paul, or else I should leave. Now when I referred to this, he said, "No, you cannot call them." Then, "Okay, you can call Roy, but only after I talk with him. And he won't be on your side, Judy. He's going to support me."

I replied, "Okay, Jim, but I want to do what I said I'd do—inform Roy that I'm worried about you."

Then he drove away. I think he was escaping from the look in my eyes that reflected how very strange he seemed to me.

I wrote in my journal right after he left: "What is scariest is that this cannot be fixed with apologies. There is no way he can instantly be back to his other self. It's something else, and I have no experience here at all. I am in such unknown territory, out of my league. Jim's implying that it's me, that I need medicine because I keep setting him off. He feels unsafe with me, seeing and feeling my scare and grief."

I called Roy, and he understood, having experienced his own alarm during a phone call with Jim the day before. He felt strongly that Jim should come be with him in Ohio. I told Roy I was afraid that my attitude toward Jim, my thinking that he was behaving bizarrely, was insulting to him. It was still too impossible to believe, and my confidence in my perception was shaky. Roy reassured me. "Everything we are doing is with Jim's best interest in mind, Judy. We want to protect him."

Roy and I did not discuss trying to hospitalize Jim for several reasons. First, we both knew that Jim would never have gone voluntarily. Secondly, I could not imagine calling the police to come get him. It was too horrifying, and I believed (and still believe) he never would have forgiven me. It had been his first instruction to me. Thirdly, Jim probably could have talked a judge into releasing him.

I did not sleep at all that night. The next morning, I waited and waited at the restaurant, but Jim never showed. At last I went home, and hours later, he finally called, coldly saying that he'd be over the next morning at nine. Then he called again later that night, upset and crying, needing reassurance. I had a glimmer of hope.

But the next day, he was cold again. He arrived at noon. I hugged him, and he was a rigid stick. As best as I remember, and it is likely pretty close because I wrote this down as soon as he drove away, our dialogue went as follows:

Judy: I was worried.

Jim: It's noon.

Judy: You said about nine or ten.

Jim: Well, it's noon. I'll take care of the trailer now. You'll have to get out. I'm going to Nashville to see Jerry [his former colleague who was dying].

Judy: What do you mean?

Jim: Are you playing fucking dumb with me again? You and my ex-wife . . . Do you want to take care of the trailer?

Judy: We can leave it here. I thought we'd return here.

Jim: Yeah? Well, you thought wrong.

Judy: You're driving to Nashville?

Jim: Yeah. What did you think, I was going to fucking walk there?

Judy: I think you need to be with your brother.

Jim: Well, too bad.

Judy: What about our stuff in the trailer?

Jim: It'll end up back in Texas, who knows when.

Judy: Well, why do you have the right to take the truck and leave me stranded? It's half mine.

Jim: Too bad. You need a ride, I'll arrange it.

Judy: I can't get out this fast. I'm staying in the trailer until Tuesday. [It was then Sunday.]

Jim: No—twenty-four hours. But that's all. You can find other places to stay.

Jim began packing, and I went out to the truck to get some things. He came out yelling for me to get out of the truck.

Jim: Get out. I have things in there.

Judy: Well, I need some things. It's my truck, too.

Jim: Well, you can only get in there with me there. [He was probably hiding marijuana.]

Judy: Fine. [I returned to the trailer.]

Jim: Well, I called the restaurant, and they knew you were going to return there at 10 A.M.

Judy: They couldn't have. I never was going to.

Jim: Shut up. Do you want to hear what I have to say or not?

Judy: Yes.

Jim: See, that just about sent me over the edge.

Judy: Well, I can understand that.

Jim: Do you want to swap a doll for that photo I gave you last week?

Judy: No. I didn't know it was a swap.

Jim: Well, it is now. You can't have it.

Judy: You're not wearing your wedding ring.

Jim: [Angry, almost spitting] It's safe. Don't worry, I'm married.

Judy: I need my sewing machine and guitar in Texas.

Jim: Well, you've got a problem, don't you?

And he drove away. That was August 24, 1996. I did not see Jim again until late November, Thanksgiving weekend.

Thus ended our summer in Washington and thus began the next horrible year.

6

THE BAD YEAR BEGINS

This next twelve months from August 1996 to August 1997, I call "The Bad Year." I never in a million years thought Jim's mania would go on that long. Everything I was reading and everyone I talked to, which included mental health professionals as well as people who were manic-depressive themselves, spoke of untreated mania as lasting three to six months. But Jim's mania went on and on.

After Jim exploded out of our life together on August 24, he traveled for about six weeks visiting family and friends, leaving chaos and shattered relationships in his wake. He stayed very active and on the move. In the first seven months of The Bad Year, Jim put some 60,000 miles on our truck before it fell apart due to his frenetic driving and lack of attention to maintenance.

To his credit, over the course of that year, Jim did some good work organizing the Clean Air for Big Bend project for the area near our Texas home, writing long articles and attending meetings. He also immersed himself in his photography, taking and developing thousands of photographs. It continually confused me that Jim seemed so productive when he was supposedly mentally ill. I could not reconcile how he could think so unclearly about me and so clearly about his work.

Anyone suggesting to Jim that he was anything less than fine, even the simplest question, "How are you, Jim?" would make him harsh and defensive. With a person who thinks he has the Answers to the Universe, confrontation or the implication that he is not okay are both useless and senseless.

That entire year I spoke of Jim as "different," not sick, partly in my determination to stay respectful of him and partly due to my buying into Jim's own assessment of himself, which led to my confusion as to whether he was, indeed, actually sick. His persuasiveness seemed to jam my own sense of what was happening. I often felt less than fully sane. Jim's ability to continue to function despite being so "different" threatened my reality over and over, eroding my confidence in my judgment and damaging my ability to trust my own perceptions.

One example of this occurred about a week after Jim left Washington, when I knew he was stopping to see his brother, Roy, and sister Cass in Ohio. I was talking with Roy and Cass daily, but I was so confused by Jim's verbal bashings that I was seriously worried they would see Jim as credible and me as a horrible wife with mental problems.

I called Cass at a prearranged time for her to tell me how things had gone with Jim's visit. I was incredibly nervous and full of dread, but I need not have worried. Jim's mental illness was unmistakable to both her and Roy. Cass saw clearly that Jim was manic, out of control, scary, and on the run. She reported that his thoughts and ideas were disconnected, jumping from one to another. She described him as brash and inflated and told me that he had gotten into huge screaming blowups with Roy and their father. She was afraid to let her children go driving with him. From then on, I relied heavily on Cass and Roy's perceptions. which did not waiver as mine did from the certainty that Jim was sick.

I stayed with my brother and his family in Hawaii for two months, not sure where to be or what to do while Jim was driving around the country. I searched for information about manic-depression, reading everything I could find. There was much information on depression, but precious little about dealing with someone who is manic. However, in the phone book, I found a listing for the Mental Health Association. One call brought me in touch with the wife and daughter of a man who was manic-depressive. These two women helped me develop a list of things to remember, which I read to myself every morning.

1. Jim is sick.
2. It is likely he will get well.
3. It is not me.
4. He had to leave because I would have asked him to come down from his high.

Through these two women, I met another woman, prominent in the community, who was manic-depressive herself and on lithium. She was separated from her husband, who was also manic-depressive, but off lithium. He had taken himself off several times over their years together, becoming manic each time, then plunging into suicidal depression. This was his fourth manic episode. It finally seemed pointless to stay with him. She was taking lithium to avoid living with cycling, and here she was, living with her husband's cycling instead.

"A person who is manic gets so willful, like the temper tantrum of a child. You can't get in their way," she told me. Her husband had spent lots of money frivolously that summer and instead of dealing with it, had told her, "Who cares? It's your problem, not mine." Among other things, she advised me to protect our money as much as possible.

She said that I must face the fact that, of course, this will recur. Manic-depression is a chronic illness. She thought that it was the hardest of any illness to deal with because:

1. It is a medical illness with a psychological expression.
2. They have a ball while they are destroying us who love them.
3. The illness is too seductive—they want it.

She advised me to respond to Jim, but not to specifics because then I would just be entering into his drama and fantasy of what reality is. Her husband had managed to function in society, but if you asked certain questions, it would trigger his craziness. She was relieved not to be trying to figure it all out anymore.

"Here's the bottom line, Judy. I don't know what you could have done better this past summer. I'm smart, and

I'm bipolar—I should have been able to figure this out. That was my quest, to know how to deal with my husband. And I couldn't do it."

And finally, "Somehow or other, Judy, you ended up on this island just when my husband is also manic, and I'm struggling to deal with it. It's something that only you and I could understand, and I feel very privileged to be helping you."

Often during The Bad Year, people whose lives were touched in one way or another by manic-depressive illness seemed to drop out of the blue. One evening at a dinner, Joe, one of my brother's friends, in Hawaii revealed to me that he was on lithium for manic-depression.

The timing of meeting Joe was remarkable. Just that morning, for the umpteenth time, Joe's wife had been urging him to stop taking lithium, telling him that he should be strong, that it was just a question of mind over body. Joe felt that if he followed her wish, it could very possibly kill him.

Now that I've learned that the tendency to stop medication is part of the illness of manic-depression, it is, indeed mind blowing that in this case, the wife was urging her husband *off* medication rather than *on*. Joe was adamant about staying on lithium. He was grateful to have the lithium, much as Jim had been before becoming manic. Joe was sure that he never wanted to be symptomatic again—it was all pain to him. He had never experienced the exhilarating high that Jim was experiencing, but only intense pressure and paranoia. "I never want to go through that again or be that crazy again. It's frightening to feel so pressured from inside yourself."

My story was immensely eye-opening to them that things could get so out of control. They were "closeted" in the little community where they lived, where Joe was trying to succeed in his private practice as a doctor. His psychiatrist was his only confidante; he had no peer group.

Joe and I met to talk several times during my weeks in Hawaii. It was a profound experience for both of us. For me, it was like talking with Jim when he was healthy, talks Jim and I had about his past and his hurts. For Joe, it was a chance to be open about his illness and his fears for himself. He told me, "Judy, God put you here at the right time for me and for my marriage."

Although he was concerned that he had little to offer, Joe tried very hard to counsel me. I urged him to help me know how to live this life that had become a science-fiction story.

Joe advised me to stay away from Jim as he was then. He said I should take care of myself and not participate in Jim's madness or his wish to crush me. He urged me to not read anything Jim wrote to me. "Don't even open his letters. They are only from his mania."

Joe thought that Jim had probably felt rejected during the summer and that it had scared him. "Jim is so dependent on you, Judy, and this is unbearable to him." Joe had always felt terribly dependent on his wife, that their relationship was unequal because she could speak of separation without the enormity of his kind of fear of being alone. "Without her, I might have another breakdown."

Joe's main message for me was this: "Jim is manic, exhibiting classic behavior. Protect your assets, Judy. And don't give up on him. He will come crawling, wanting you back, wanting you to forgive him. Jim is manic-depressive, Judy. He will cycle."

What I appreciated so much about Joe was that he really knew how painful this was. And like many others I met that year, he wanted to make up for the pain his illness had caused others by helping another victim of the devastation of manic-depressive illness, i.e., me.

Another woman I met in Hawaii hadn't been diagnosed until five years after her highs and lows began, by which time her husband had left her, unable to deal with her moods. Her children blamed her and still kept their distance from her. Once she was diagnosed, she started taking lithium, and it helped immensely. Until she stopped taking it.

This was a beautiful, centered, well-spoken, fifty-year-old woman; I was startled to hear about her many messes. Her last manic episode had been only three years earlier when she'd been trying various types of alternative healing. She'd felt good and had stopped lithium. Immediately, her life fell into ruins.

She told me, "Each episode I have ends up being a year and a half I lose out of my life. Of course I wish I could keep some of the high feeling and associations my mind can do when I'm high. It would help my writing. But when I'm manic, I can focus and follow through on nothing. In the end, I need to be on lithium."

She advised me to stay away from Jim so that I would not accumulate more negative memories of him. "Jim will have to earn the right to have your relationship again. He will have to come with remorse, apologies, amends."

And, like Joe, she cautioned me to protect our financial assets.

Money was a lot of the focus of Jim's fury at me during The Bad Year. At the urging of our friends and families that I be realistic about Jim being manic, I made two financial changes. Both felt disrespectful toward Jim and were very difficult for me to do.

Early on, as the credit card bills were coming in for Jim's travels from Washington State to Nashville, back to Washington, then to Texas, reflecting thousands of miles of gasoline, motels, and restaurants, I began to worry. It is common knowledge that a person who is manic can go through a lot of money and ring up a lot of bills. The criteria for diagnosis of a manic episode in manic-depressive illness, as described in the *Diagnostic and Statistical Manual (DSM IV)*, include "excess involvement in pleasurable activities that have a high potential for painful consequences (e.g., engaging in unrestrained buying sprees . . . or foolish business investments)." In their book, *Synopsis of Psychiatry*, Kaplan and Sadock emphasize it even more. "Impaired judgment is a hallmark of manic patients. They may break laws regarding credit cards . . . and finances, sometimes involving their families in financial ruin."

Of a more personal nature was something Kay Redfield Jamison wrote in her autobiographical book, *An Unquiet Mind*:

> When I am high I couldn't worry about money if I tried . . . I imagine I must have spent far more than thirty thousand dollars during my two

major manic episodes. . . But then back on lithium and rotating on the planet at the same pace
as everyone else, you find your credit is decimat-
ed, your mortification complete: mania is not a
luxury one can easily afford.

The first thing I did was to take away Jim's ability to
charge things. Since the credit card was in my name, it
was simple to cancel it. I told Jim I would be doing this
before I actually did it so that he would not be caught
off guard in the midst of a purchase. He was outraged
since he saw none of his spending as excessive. He
insisted, "You should want to pay for my expenses, after
how you treated me during the summer." I wish I could
say that I knew this was crazy thinking on his part, but
in my confusion at the time, I wondered whether he
might be right. Still, I stuck to my plan.

The second thing I did was to contact the investment
companies where we had joint accounts and ask that
they require both our names in order to cash any investments held jointly. In addition to our joint moneys, Jim
and I had separate accounts so this was not going to
leave him financially stranded. But he was furious and
said I was being underhanded. Part of me agreed with
him; I felt slimy doing it. But I had to allow for the possibility that those who advised me to do this could be
right, and I had to believe that I was trying to protect
Jim from some of the consequences of his mania.

As it turned out, Jim did not spend wildly during
that year. But he did spend about four times what his
army disability check covered and so was draining his
own savings.

I believe that Jim's anger at me over these money issues was mostly because he realized that my actions were prompted by my belief that he was manic. He did not like this mirror and sought to smash it.

Needing to be somewhere familiar, I left Hawaii in October and went back to Nashville, where I spent the next ten months among friends. I kept waiting for all of this to end. Jim was supposed to crash into depression and be willing to get back on medication because, after all, manic-depression is a cycling illness. In a state of suspension, I could not make myself do anything permanent—I lived waiting for a phone call.

When I compared myself to Jim's energy and productiveness, I felt like a slug. In retrospect, it might have been better for me to have done something differently, something with more routine that provided ongoing structure. Perhaps I should have gotten a job of some sort, something to fill my time, something I could have put down easily if and when Jim needed me.

I did what I could. Once a week, I worked on the Neonatal Intensive Care Unit at Vanderbilt Hospital as a "cuddler," holding the tiny babies. Sad to say, touch was probably as important and soothing to me as it was to them. Later, I volunteered a few days a week on a construction crew that was building a wildlife park in Nashville. It was good for me to be outdoors doing physical labor, seeing tangible results. I also continued to volunteer with the Red Cross by assisting at a flood in western Tennessee.

Music filled much of my time. I took guitar lessons and played with friends. Although it was difficult to concentrate, I continued to write my songs. For exercise, I ran, having been a jogger for twenty years.

What I could concentrate on best was my journal and the daily chronicle of the ongoing nightmare, writing that became the basis for this book. Describing the details of events as they were occurring helped me to get from one day to the next.

One of the things that I got bogged down in was Jim's assertion that his unmedicated self was his "real" self. In his book, *Electroboy: A Memoir of Mania,* Andy Behrman writes:

> Plainly, I will never be able to stop taking these medications. Am I more myself on them or less? There's no sense in trying to determine which me is the real me—in the end, I need the medications if I'm to lead a balanced life. I have a chronic illness, and I can't survive without them.

If I heard Jim say "this is the real me" once that year, I heard him say it dozens of times. Manic-depressive illness is like an acid. It eats away at memories and reality. Once Jim was high, his view of everyone changed. Compared to his own extreme state, everyone else seemed depressed. This included me, and this included him prior to June 1996, the self who took lithium. In declaring, "This is the *real* me," Jim was insisting that I had only known him as a depressed person, that he had been depressed ever since I had met him. "Furthermore," he would spit at me, "you obviously prefer me depressed."

But the Jim I had known for nine years had not been

depressed. Quite the opposite—Jim had confirmed many times that it was the best he had ever felt. He was correct in that there was no question that I preferred that other Jim, the one who took his four pink capsules every day. This other man was not someone to whom I would ever have chosen to be married.

In describing his unmedicated self as his "real" self, Jim blithely skipped over the fact that he was now self-medicating with marijuana, caffeine, nicotine, and alcohol, as well as various herbs and "natural remedies." He could not see the logic that lithium is as natural as anything, being merely a salt. His thinking was too scrambled to remember the analogy that is often made to diabetes. That is, without insulin the diabetic would be unmedicated and yes, natural, his or her "real" self; but he or she would also be dead.

If Jim had met another woman and fallen out of love with me, I could have coped somehow. Losing a husband to the proverbial "blonde in the office" I had already done with my first husband. I knew how to do that one. Not pleasant, but, much like an illness, it runs one of several predictable courses: He leaves, he stays gone, gets remarried; or he leaves, he gets jilted, returns. And so on.

It also has reference materials, novels, poems, plays, songs. The story is as old as time. But mania, this terribly complicated and foreign puzzle just kept me perpetually off balance. Manic-depression is a unique illness in the way it causes such sudden change in a person. Loved ones are caught off guard with no comparable experiences on which to draw. The matter of where the

rest of his feelings and personality were perpetually tortured me. Were they dissolved and gone forever? Were
they only buried under the avalanche of the mania, and
if so, then I wondered whether his essential "Jim-ness"
could be dug out.

As time went by, I doubted more and more that this
was the case. Different as Jim had become, it did not
seem possible that his original self could still exist. I,
too, began to question what was his "real" self when the
Jim I had known for nine-and-a-half years had been his
medicated self.

The perspective that I found most helpful about mania,
I did not find until after Jim had died. Katherine
Graham's book, *Personal History*, was published sometime in 1997, possibly before Jim's death, but I did not
come across it until 1998. In it, she gives a detailed history of her fifteen-year marriage to her husband, Phil,
his manic-depressive illness years before lithium was
being used, his mania, and then his suicide in 1962.

Phil's manic-depressive illness emerged slowly over
their years together, mostly diagnosed as episodes of
depression. The several manic episodes that came later
sounded remarkably like Jim's, full of blame of
Katherine and adoration of another woman.

She writes of his manic episodes:

> . . . the apparently normal encounters Phil was
> having with others shook me—about him, and
> about us. Was this the real Phil? And was this
> what he really wanted? . . .What he seemed to be
> saying was that whatever was the matter with
> him was my fault.

Katherine Graham's responses to her husband's manic behavior were so similar to mine, thereby helping to normalize much of what I had been feeling. This strengthened me and made me feel less crazy. Unfortunately, Jim was dead by then.

Some of the hardest times during that year were when people casually said about Jim, "He seems fine to me." To quote Katherine Graham again:

> The most painful moments—the ones that disturbed me the most profoundly—were those in which people reported to me that they had seen Phil and that he appeared to be rational and calm, indeed quite well.

Each time someone said this to me, it would not only make me feel crazy and doubt my perceptions, it also made me very sad. To me, it meant that Jim was being able to share himself with others and was not alienated from everyone as he was alienated from me. I missed him so much, it was hard to bear.

But Jim did seem fine at certain times to certain people. It is a fact that a person who is manic may seem or actually be in control of himself—in the present. However, he is not in control of the bigger picture. He has forgotten that depression is waiting and that he is almost inevitably headed for disaster.

The months went by with Jim able to construct a life separate from me. He remained convinced that he was fine and had found his real self.

7

FAMILY AND FRIENDS

I do not think I would have survived the year without the support of our friends and families. At the same time, they were an enormous source of tension between Jim and me and raised constant issues about loyalty.

People who were close to both of us knew what was happening. But those who were not our close friends, specifically our neighbors on the ranch we were part of in Texas, were uninformed. In October 1996, still at the beginning of The Bad Year, as Jim was returning to our home in Texas after his six-week trip around the country, his brother and sister and I confided in one of our Texas neighbors about Jim's manic-depressive illness. We felt someone nearby should be informed about the risk of depression and suicide if and when Jim's mania ended, and she was our closest neighbor. This person seemed savvy and concerned. Unfortunately, however, confiding in her turned out to be a mistake, as she chose to tell Jim about our call, which of course enraged him and led to more of his venom.

I told no one else in Texas about Jim's illness. Since Jim had returned to our casita and I had not, I did not think it right for me to breach his privacy by telling neighbors that he was manic-depressive and off medication. I was trying to be respectful of Jim, trying to protect his privacy. Jim was explaining my absence to them and to himself by saying that I was depressed over my father's death the previous January. I did not contact these neighbors to counter this. I did not tell them that Jim was not allowing me to come near him.

Consequently, people in Texas only had whatever information Jim provided plus what they observed in his behavior. Our neighbors knew Jim was acting differently than he had in the three years they had known him, but most thought he must be using cocaine, which to them explained his volatile, accelerated behavior. It was only at his memorial that they learned differently.

I was fortunate that many of my friends were also therapists, and I leaned heavily on them all year. So many kindnesses were shown to me. People devoted huge amounts of time to just listening to me, repetitive though I was. One friend, Stanley, took me on a trip to Prague as a diversion and gift. A friend of a friend, Sadie, who barely knew me, let me stay ten months at her home in Nashville while I waited for Jim to crash.

I sought out friends who were dealing with manic-depression. Years before I had learned that a friend's physician-husband was manic-depressive. At that time, this was merely an interesting fact. Now I thought of her again, hoping she could help me. We met only once, and it was a difficult meeting.

She told me that her husband, who had been hospitalized three times, was taking lithium and Thorazine, but that he wanted not to take any medications, to just stay high. She told me she was frightened of what her husband sometimes did when he was manic and especially of how inappropriately he sometimes acted with his patients. In the past, he had given money to them and had also handed out cash to strangers on the street.

She said she always tried to flow where her husband flowed and tried to stay in sync with him so she could advise him about his medications. When he would get a little high, she would tell him he needed more Thorazine. Her leverage was his work, which he loved. (I had no such leverage since Jim was not accountable to any work situation.)

She believed there was nothing I could do from twelve hundred miles away, that I should live in Alpine, the closest town to our casita. Although still two hours away, I would be close enough to try to influence Jim to take medication. I could also look for openings to work on our marriage.

She also felt that, since Jim would not take medication, I should brainstorm with his family how to drug him heavily for two weeks while we gave him lithium. She told me about her neighbor whose manic-depressive husband was beating her, so she began putting Haldol, an antipsychotic medicine, in his orange juice. My friend thought that this was a great idea and added, "Who cares about 'civil rights' when it's your husband's mind and well-being that are at stake?"

But I felt the risk was too great, that if Jim discovered what I was doing, he would hate me even more. I could even imagine him trying to have me arrested for violating him.

Other friends said that they would like to tie Jim down and force-feed medicine into him. They were quite serious. But I was stuck in my fear, both then and later, of taking whatever risks might be necessary in order to stand firm or try to coerce Jim. Jim had instructed me, "Do not try to contain me yourself." I was afraid he would hate me when he got well. In their textbook, *Manic-Depressive Illness*, Goodwin and Jamison describe it this way: "The spouse feels trapped in an impossible situation, caught in a whirlwind of activity, personally threatened, powerless to enforce limits."

After we left on our Getaway in 1993, a friend of Jim's who was also diagnosed with manic-depressive illness had a manic episode, soon followed by a horrible depression. During The Bad Year, although it was painful for her, this man's wife agreed to meet with me. She described her husband during his manic episode as "cold as ice," uninterested in her or what might hurt her. She said that at times he seemed actually intent on hurting her emotionally just to show he could do it and not care, to show how he had the upper hand. It sounded a lot like Jim's behavior.

Then came her husband's depression, which plunged him into the depths of despair and helplessness. She said he became like a child, and she had to care for him as someone who needed guidance and soothing and structure. This was awful for her, treating her husband as less than the capable man he had always been. But she was loyal and determined.

When her husband recovered, he felt concerned for Jim and visited him in Texas. As I remember it, his report was that Jim seemed fine, out and about and building a life for himself. This, of course, was confusing and painful for me to hear. All I can figure is that Jim did seem fine to him. I suppose it is possible that Jim was covering well or perhaps this friend was idealizing what appeared to be Jim's "freedom," especially his freedom from medication.

At last report, this man was stable. His wife tells me that they finally reached out to friends, that his manic-depressive illness is not the secret it had been, which is certainly important. By mutual agreement, she monitors her husband's behavior and has tremendous influence on his staying on medication because he knows that if he stops, she will leave him and take their children. They also have a psychiatrist they trust, whom they see together and who reminds them that medical decisions in their case will be based primarily on the wife's perspective.

As for a plan, I told her a suggestion that was made by several people I had spoken with who themselves were diagnosed. Their idea was for the person to make a video of himself while healthy, advising his friends and family how to deal with him if he were to become manic. Unfortunately, when manic again, it is likely he would attribute such a tape to "I was sedated when I made that tape" or "I was just doing it to keep people off my back—it was my strategy."

A person who is manic is amazingly skillful at rationalizing and rewriting history.

Another friend told me that his mother had many manic episodes during his childhood.

"Sometimes I didn't know who this was. Where had my mother gone? Then sometimes, maybe five years at a stretch, she was better, more able to be a mom."

He and I talked about this late one night at a street fair outside Nashville, rock music blasting, both of us crying.

"One time she wanted soup, so I made her soup. I was probably about nineteen at the time. I took the soup up to her room and handed it to her. She took the soup and flung it onto the floor."

He went on. "Then she got down on her hands and knees, on all fours, and began eating the soup off the floor, like a dog." He shook his head. "I had to leave. I left the house and didn't come back for a week or more. I couldn't.

"She got on lithium in the sixties when it was still experimental, but they always had trouble with her dosages. Also, as she aged, what would be a therapeutic dose changed, and all along, that fine line between therapeutic dose and toxic level was difficult to walk for her.

"You know, Judy, however horrible it is for us, I believe it's worse for them." He got teary again. "My mother would get high for three weeks, a month, and she never said, 'Hey, it's January 20. Where did December 11 go and all this time?' We never talked about it. It was never mentioned at all. But what must that have felt like for her—the confusion, the shame? She painted and sculpted when she was high, and she was very creative and talented then. But she would change, and I would have no mother."

All of these stories made me feel less alone.

Early on in The Bad Year, when these chance meet-ings and conversations took place, I saw them as omens, possible turning points, perhaps even signs from God. They were too profound to be mere coincidence. But by the time of this last conversation, there had been so many disappointments and false alarms that I no longer took them as signs or omens. Still, this was an impor-tant conversation, and it brought yet another instanta-neous closeness with someone who knew the terrain of the planet on which I was living.

The individuality of the illness was apparent and how it manifested itself so varied. However, the havoc it wreaked on the manic person's family and friends was very much the same.

Jim celebrated his fiftieth birthday during The Bad Year, on November 1, 1996. On top of my daily sorrow, it was additionally awful not to be celebrating with him. But in Jim's world, a wonderful thing happened on this particular birthday: He reconciled with his sons, then twenty-eight and twenty-two years old.

They had not spoken nor written to one another for three years, way before Jim stopped taking lithium. We had last seen his older son when we left on our Getaway in May 1993. We had seen his younger son in June 1993 when the three of us visited Carlsbad Cavern. There was a letter or two over the next few months, but after that, Jim had no contact with either of them.

Jim had been angry at both of them. He had felt that he was having to do all the initiating and decided to see what would happen if he did not propel the contact. The answer was that nothing happened. There was no contact. I believed that he, as the parent, had more of the responsibility of keeping in touch, however minimally, and disagreed with his tactic. But Jim was adamant that he was not going to be the only one keeping the ball rolling in the relationship with his sons. Again, this was three years before Jim stopped taking lithium.

This cutoff persisted until his older son called Jim on his fiftieth birthday. Neither of his sons knew that Jim was off lithium and that our lives were falling apart. Jim gave them the same explanation for our separation that he gave everyone. "Judy is depressed. She spent all summer secluding herself in the trailer, making dolls."

Of course, Jim was very glad about the rapprochement with his sons. He soon told me that I was free to call them and go see them.

I did, in fact, visit each of them two months later. These were difficult meetings for me, partly because I had not seen either one for more than three years, but mostly because both of them said that they did not see anything wrong with their father. At Jim's memorial nine months later, his older son tearfully admitted he had been in denial back then, that he had just been so glad to be back in touch with his father.

My family loved Jim. Jim's family loved me. This was an enormous tragedy for all of them. My brother adored Jim. Jim telephoned him and all my cousins with whom I am very close, sure they would all accept his take on the situation, that I was depressed since my father's death. But, of course, they did not. Jim was harsh, insistent, and demanding in a way they had never experienced him before, which confirmed what I had told them. Also, my cousins knew me well; they saw that I was unhappy, but the reason was evident.

Jim called my first husband wanting to commiserate about me. He asked Geoffrey whether I had also hidden from him that something was wrong with me, that I was disturbed. After telling Jim that he did not know what he was talking about, Geoffrey called me wondering what was going on. When I told him, Geoffrey's response was: "It's scary that there's someone out there with so much personal information about you, running around without the boundaries of normal common decency."

In fact, I received many calls from family members and friends wondering what was going on and asking was I depressed. As soon as I heard that, I knew that they had received a call from Jim. Jim had loved my family and in his inflated state, he felt that they would all embrace him. However, although they tried to stay open to him, they were upset with him for hurting me. It infuriated Jim that they could not see "how disturbed Judy is."

My cousins tried to reason with Jim, tried to be available to him. But Jim could not stay in contact with anyone who did not see him as absolutely fine or agree with him that I was both disturbed and wrong.

Jim's family kept me close. Jim had emotionally brutalized his father, brother, and sister during his trip around the country in September, and they had pulled back from him. Jim blamed me for the distance he felt from them, that I was turning them against him. While it was true that his brother and sister were mortified about Jim's treatment of me, it was Jim's meanness and volatility that kept them from reaching out to him directly. They never left the playing field the entire time, but dealing with Jim directly was like walking in an explosives factory.

I stayed close to Jim's family for a variety of reasons beyond my love for them. It was now the closest to Jim I could get. He insisted that it increased our distance, but I don't think this was so. He was not going to be with me, not lovingly, regardless.

Also, Roy had been part of the "fail-safe" plan Jim had outlined to me back in early July when he first announced that he was not going back on lithium. Hence, Roy had been the first person I called when Jim exploded out of our life, and this had immediately engaged his whole family. If I had not called Roy on August 24, 1996, had not at least attempted to follow the guidelines of Jim's plan, I surely would have had regrets and questioned my judgment even more than I did and still do.

Jim's oldest brother, who is bipolar, also kept in close touch with me. I stayed connected with Jim's parents, although his mother was dreadfully ambivalent about Jim's changes, being unaccepting of her own manic-depressive illness. At times during The Bad Year, she was worried about Jim. But too often her perspective was that Jim was doing exciting things and that she and he were going to be great companions, traveling together, full of projects. I could not stand to listen to this. I could not understand how she could believe that he was all right when he was being so obviously harsh and cruel to her own husband and children.

And of course, there was Jim's sister, Cass. She and

I remained very close, and she was immensely supportive of me throughout, as well as being much clearer than
I about Jim's impairment.

Jim was very sure that friends and family thought he
was fine when in reality most did not think that at all.
He would throw in my face how someone close to us was
totally supportive of his new perceptions when in actuality they had just told me that they thought that he was
off the wall. Early on in The Bad Year, a psychiatrist
friend of my brother told me that although bottom line,
I didn't have much control, I should keep reminding Jim
that he was not well even though he was feeling on top
of the world. He told me to say or write to Jim, "I love
you. I want to be with you. But you think you're fine,
and you're not fine." On his advice, I asked friends and
family to write to Jim with honest feedback.

I suppose this suggestion was a variation on the
theme of an "intervention." ("Intervention" is a term
used in the field of addictions, where those close to the
addict confront him as a group in order to push him
toward treatment.) What follow are excerpts from letters written to Jim in September and October of 1996:

From Jim's mother: "It pains me to write this letter.
But I must find out what you are doing to yourself, your
wife, your family. Are you awaiting a catastrophe? I'm
afraid I am, Jimmie, I am very sad. I feel empty as I did
when you disappeared 13 years ago."

From Jim's father: "Perhaps I should have written
this sooner. I hope it's not too late. To me, Jim, you are
on a 'high road' headed for a crash . . . You must get
back on medication before you dig yourself a hole you

can't crawl out of. You say your family supports what you are doing. I don't get that sense talking to them."

From Jim's oldest brother: "The big bone of contention is lithium, and as you know I stand with those that think you should be on it . . . Finally, the big thing: your 'new life.' It's pretty exciting. But there are risks. One, you might crash. Two, you might not have enough money . . . Sorry for the cliche—there's a price for everything."

From Roy, his next younger brother: "As far as I am concerned, you are and have been clearly and dramatically in the midst of a manic episode for at least a month now . . . Your clinical picture is seriously clouded by the 'mild' nature of your mania; i.e. you are not running naked down the street or anything else that would make for headlines . . . A consequence of all of this is that you are leaving, among other things, a trail of turmoil at best, destruction at worst behind you. One of your coping mechanisms seems to be to aggressively, recklessly . . . cast aspersions, doubts, and negative innuendos on anyone courageous and honest enough to share with you their genuine experience of you in the last month—i.e. there is something seriously wrong with this guy . . . The reason that I am making an attempt to keep loving you is that I know what a wonderful, kind, deep, thoughtful person you have been; and the firm belief that you are currently mentally ill and projecting shit as far and wide as you can throw it . . . Be careful—the stakes are potentially catastrophic . . . I think you have a snowball's chance in hell of keeping this going for long."

From one of my friends: "With deep respect for you, I join your parents, siblings, in-laws, and friends who see you as needing to be back on some appropriate medication . . . to regain the balance in your energy and thought processes that allows us to recognize the connecting, loving, caring Jim we all stand in support of."

From one of my cousins: "Jim, to me you're right now a guy who's traveling down the highway at 100 miles an hour . . . Judy is frightened for you, and so am I, Jim. I'm going to tell you flat out that this 100 mile an hour stuff may look fine to you, but you're not driving well. You're agitated, aggressive, and obstinate in a faulty belief that you're in control of this vehicle. You're not. You're careening out of control. Where's it going to end up? Jim, obviously the most difficult part of this conundrum is that intrinsic to your problem is your inability to see your problem. So please give some credence to the people who care about you. We're not stupid, we're not manipulated, we're not assholes. We care.... It may, good buddy, save your life."

These letters, of course, infuriated Jim, and he adeptly discounted each one. When all was said and done, all that the letters served to do was to alienate Jim from all these people to one degree or another. Nonetheless, I did not and do not regret that people sent them. Given how things turned out, I think I would have regretted if I had not at least tried this barrage of feedback.

The person who felt the pain most like I did was Jim's best friend in Nashville, Paul. Naturally, his pain was of a lesser degree because he was a friend, not a spouse, and also he had already had to deal with losing Jim when we moved to Texas. Consequently, Paul did not personalize Jim's behavior and projections as I did.

Paul and Jim had been best friends for the whole six years we lived in Nashville, and they stayed in close contact after we moved away. They both enjoyed being up-to-date with current events and loved to challenge one another's opinions. More importantly, they were confidants, sharing intimate details of their lives with one another.

Jim trashed Paul during The Bad Year because Paul questioned Jim's judgment. He was horrid to Paul, trivializing their relationship and only seeing him if Paul would abide by Jim's rules. Paul had stories similar to mine of Jim's aggressive behavior, such as when Jim threatened to scream in a fancy restaurant in Nashville in December, the threat hissed through clenched teeth. I knew it all too well.

Paul mourned, but kept an internal steadiness that I could not. He reminded himself over and over and over again, "This is not Jim talking. This Jim is ill. This is not happening because of a lack in me or something I've done, much as Jim blames me. Jim is mentally ill."

Being with Paul helped me immensely. The first time we spoke, soon after my return to Nashville in October, it was immediately obvious that, like myself, Paul was injured. Jim had called Paul with an invitation to come to Texas for his fiftieth birthday party. "I'm having a wingding," Jim told him. When Paul had not immediately agreed to come, Jim had responded with a threat: "If you don't come, I will consider our friendship over."

Paul was terribly disturbed and needed to talk, which we did. Hearing his stories made me feel a little less crazy. Paul also had a lot of energy to listen to me. I told him how I blamed myself, how I was feeling I had done nothing to help the situation. I should have done x, I should have done y, etc. Paul's responses were always comforting and often amazing, and I wrote down many of them in my journal:

"You've been deliberate in staying away from Jim. You've been trying to be respectful of his guideline, 'Do not try to contain me. Call Roy and clear out.'"

"If a military leader does his best strategies and is very competent and yet in the battle many of his men die, he cannot say, 'I should have taken that other course, etc.' He did his best with the information he had."

"Mr. Jacobson is in the cattle car on the train to Auschwitz. It does him no good to say, 'I should have been friendlier to my neighbors.' It would not have mattered."

"It is a form of self-inflation, Judy, for you to think you could have made a difference when this is beyond others' scope."

"Judy, you do so well. You got information, you've hung in, you've tried to love him, to reach out, to be with him. No one could have done better."

"You wouldn't want this Jim."

"Jim left due to a chemical change that made him unbearable to those who loved him."

"Jim took medicine that blessedly gave him a life of contentment and miracles. He chose to get off the medicine, and this is who he has become."

8

CODEPENDENCY OR LOVE?

Jim and I saw each other five times between August 24, 1996, when he drove away and left our life, and August 13, 1997, when he asked me to return to him. We had horrible talks on the phone that always resulted in his screaming at me. In addition to these calls, Jim wrote many rageful, accusatory letters to me.

All year, Jim maintained that I had initiated the separation by not returning to our home in Texas in October when he did. He totally ignored the fact that on August 24, he had taken off his wedding ring, screamed at me, and driven away, leaving me stranded at our trailer.

I wanted desperately to be with Jim and went to him every time he asked me. But each time I was near him, his fury shoved me away, and I was devastated as he flaunted what he claimed were his new romantic exploits. I went to him, but it felt like voluntarily putting my hand in a food chopper.

Our first face-to-face encounter was over Thanksgiving weekend in Washington, D.C., where we usually gathered with my cousins for the holiday. Jim had arranged to stay with his own cousins there, and we saw each other two days in a row for a few hours each time.

The visits were a mess. I met Jim's plane at the airport, which he had not expected, and he was angry about that. He was dressed differently than I had ever seen him—his sparse hair was pulled back into a small ponytail, he wore a leather hat and a necklace and bracelet. He was too thin. But then, so was I, and he told me he did not find my thinness attractive.

He barely let me touch him and would not touch me. He refused to talk with me at all unless I agreed that I had "violated his civil rights," so I went along with this. Both days, I acquiesced to much of what Jim said, some out of confusion and some in an effort to create an atmosphere that would allow us to reunite.

It really did not matter what I said or did. Whatever small gains we may have made all blew up when he went back to Texas. He found new things to accuse me of, and once again, there was nothing but harshness and distance between us.

Our next meeting took place in December. Jim called me one night to tell me that he had come to the conclusion that he now considered us "spiritually divorced." He said that this allowed him to feel separate, so he could now imagine me coming to Texas and perhaps we could even write together.

This made no sense to me, but I was longing to see

Jim, still deeply hoping that we could find a way to be together. On a more practical note, I also needed to get one of our vehicles to use. My friend Mary had generously been loaning her car to me, and she needed it back. So I flew down to Texas.

Jim met me at the airport. We hugged briefly, but as soon as we got in the truck, he began yelling at me for all I was putting him through. As we drove, he demanded that I listen to a tape he had made three months earlier on his trip away from me. The five-hour drive back to our house was filled with this nonstop raging commentary on how I had mistreated him and how I was continuing to dishonor him. I tried to stay calm, to take his feelings seriously, despite the out-of-control way he was expressing them.

I suppose I was desperately hoping that if I could accept his feelings, he would be open to me. But upon arrival at our house, he immediately insisted that he could not be in my presence, and he drove off into the night. I later learned that he went three hours down the road to the home of a woman he was seeing.

He called me the next morning, wanting me to meet him at a restaurant about an hour from the house so that we could go take photographs. We spent a strained day together, at the end of which he returned me to the Jeep, suddenly furious with me for not tipping someone as much as he thought I should have. Once again, he raced off in the truck. I didn't know what was happening or where he had gone. All I could think to do was to drive back to the casita in the Jeep.

As I drove down the highway, there was Jim parked by the side of the road. He waved for me to pull over, and my heart leaped that maybe he had calmed down. I was amazingly naive, a grotesque version of Charlie Brown with Lucy. As soon as I pulled over, Jim ferociously punched the plastic windows of the Jeep, screaming at me that I was "spiritually sick," insisting that he could not be in a relationship with me unless I gave away all my money and disowned all my friends. He screeched off in the truck, and the rest of the so-called "visit" I spent alone and in despair, trying to reconcile myself to the obvious. After several days of wondering what to do, I drove our Jeep back to Nashville, utterly hopeless.

The next would-be visit was in January 1997. After the December visit, Jim had become more frenzied, issuing threats and ultimatums. There was even a period of days when it appeared that Jim was spinning farther out of control, when his brother, sister, parents, and I thought we might be able to intervene and actually have him hospitalized.

But then out of nowhere, I received a calm and coherent letter from Jim wanting me to assist him at our home in Texas with a get-together he was having for his Clean Air for Big Bend project. "Let's get some resolution," he wrote. "Come be here with me for a month. Then come with me to my Santa Fe photography workshop."

This invitation, coming after many threats that he was going to file for divorce, jolted and confused me. But once again, I somehow found a way to make myself believe something good might come of it.

I did at least exert some caution. Instead of biting off the whole month in one chunk, I flew down and rented a car for just the weekend. If things went well, I would drive back down in the Jeep.

Indeed, within minutes of me arriving at our house, Jim read a letter he had written to me that morning, announcing that he had changed his mind and did not want me to come to Santa Fe with him after all. Then, a few hours later, he screamed at me about money again and locked me out of the house. The next day, he drove away, and again I spent the "visit" alone.

We met again in February when Jim drove to Nashville to retrieve some of his belongings from our storage. I helped him load our truck, which we did peacefully. But as soon as we were finished, he became furious with me for something and drove off, screaming out the window that he would not be seeing anymore of me.

I learned later that he had a lover in Nashville and that he went to her place.

The fifth and last time that I saw Jim before he asked me to return to him was in July 1997 when I went with a moving truck to pick up my belongings from our Texas home. Jim had already filed for divorce, and I felt that it was time for me to face the music.

During The Bad Year, there were several times when I thought something might be changing and that there might be hope. I came to call these "false alarms." What I was looking for was a sign that the supposedly inevitable had happened, an arrest, a hospitalization, some sort of trouble that would force Jim to get treatment. Failing that, I hoped for the plunge into depression that would signal that his manic cycle was over, which would likely make him amenable to medication.

One of these false alarms happened when Jim first returned to the casita in October 1996. Someone I knew at the ranch told me that Jim had gotten into a big fight with another person and the police were almost called. I was excited—if he were brought into custody, maybe he would explode and be hospitalized. I called Jim's brother and sister, and we were on pins and needles for a few days. But as time passed and nothing further happened, it became apparent that this was useless wishing.

With the combination of Jim's driving and his drinking and marijuana use, his family and I thought for sure he would get in an accident in which the police would be called or he would get stopped and possibly arrested. But it never happened. In fact, Jim bragged about this to us, citing this as proof that he was not sick or out of control and certainly not manic.

The climax of these false alarms came at the beginning of January 1997, when Jim, six months off lithium, accused Roy, Cass, and me of being involved in a conspiracy. This was so obviously paranoid thinking that it got all of us hopeful.

It began one night with Jim's 3 A.M. call to Roy, followed by numerous messages on my answering machine threatening divorce if he did not hear by 5 P.M. that I had signed papers agreeing to release our mutual investments. He also called his mother, rambling and crying.

Then there was a phone message to me stating, "If I find out that you are involved in the cover-up with Roy and Cass, Judy . . ." That's all the message said.

I called him back. "What are you talking about, Jim? What cover-up?"

"I won't say it. I'm not telling you." I had no idea what he was talking about.

It turned out that Jim believed that Roy was sexually abusing Cass's three children. He was also accusing Cass and me of being in a conspiracy to cover it up.

For two days, Jim left threatening messages on my phone, called his older brother, called his mother. He was incoherent some of the time, nonsensical at other times. His mother was at last admitting to me that she felt Jim needed to be in a hospital and on medicine. This was very significant since his mother, also manic-depressive, had previously been saying that she was enjoying Jim's energy and that they were planning on traveling together. Although she took lithium, she never accepted that she needed it. It was a big deal that she was now agreeing that Jim was ill.

We were mobilizing at last. Jim's mother wanted to know what V.A. hospitals were close to the casita. Jim's older brother felt that I should get ready to go to Texas.

But suddenly, no one heard from Jim for several days. No one had any idea where he was. Then, just as suddenly, he resurfaced and called his mother, speaking calmly and wanting to talk again about their traveling together.

What Jim told me later about that incident was that he could feel his thinking getting out of hand and knew that he was becoming delusional. He said he feared that someone would come to find him, so he had disappeared to a friend's house and laid low until he once again felt in control of his thinking.

It was a terrible disappointment to all of us. I had been down on my knees in gratitude that this nightmare might be coming to an end. When the whole thing fizzled, it drained hope from all of us who loved Jim.

I was the loving wife of a man who seemed to hate me, but whose hatred was caused and controlled by a sickness in his brain. What was the "right" thing to do? Jim was sick, and I knew that I would wait forever for him to be well again. I believe that this is love. This is loyalty and commitment. This is marriage. However, it was also true that in his illness, Jim was terribly abusive emotionally, and I was losing my strength.

I felt immensely confused about what constituted healthy behavior on my part. It was difficult to sort out whether my hanging in and waiting, which also meant subjecting myself to Jim's emotional blasts, was evidence of something good, i.e. my loyalty and commitment, or evidence of something much more self-destructive.

And loyalty to what? To a husband who was presumably mentally ill, yet whose daily life seemed more productive and forward moving than mine? He was living in the home we had just built, heavily involved in photography, and doing a substantial amount of work on the political project concerning air pollution.

As for me, I was living out of a suitcase, staying with friends, playing a little music, doing a little songwriting, but mostly desperately needing to talk, read, and write about this awful situation. I spent a lot of time crying. It was hard for me not to question whether I was being just plain stupid, deluding myself about the truth.

In his mania, Jim appeared so strong and sure. I was

waiting for the cycling into depression that would have reinforced my position; but he was not cycling.

I compared myself to wives in other situations in which their husbands had in effect disappeared, either physically or mentally. For example, a woman whose husband develops Alzheimer's has lost the man she once knew. However, she is not being weak or stupid as she hangs in with him and continues to care for him physically and emotionally. He is obviously suffering from dementia, so if he says unkind things, it is definitely the product of his withering brain. His illness is evident. She does not have to wonder whether he is being intentionally malicious, trying to control her through his knowledge of her vulnerabilities. Her belief in herself is not necessarily compromised. Also, Alzheimer's is an illness for which society accepts and applauds the caregiver taking charge and making decisions for the patient.

At times, it helped me to think about Barbara Mullen Keenan, who wrote *Every Effort*, a book about her husband's disappearance when he was shot down over Laos during the Viet Nam War. He was considered missing in action, possibly in a prisoner-of-war camp in Laos. For seven years, she waited without hearing anything definite about what had happened to him or where he was. She was being loyal and hopeful as she lived with her helplessness to effect any change. How could she just go on to enjoy her life, thinking of him held prisoner, possibly being starved, tortured?

Surely, she was much affected by this waiting and her prolonged helplessness. But her confidence in herself as a woman was not compromised. She was sure her love for her husband was pure and justified her behavior. I could not find a group of loving partners with whom I could wholly identify in order to help me sort out how to handle my feelings.

In thinking about how this all had come about, someone suggested that maybe Jim, turning fifty, was simply in the midst of a midlife crisis, needing something new in his life and from our marriage, throwing it all to the wind. The question then became did his stopping lithium trigger the midlife crisis, or did the midlife crisis cause him to stop taking lithium? This perspective hurt me as did any view that took what was happening to him and to us out of the realm of Jim's manic-depressive illness.

Jim sent me lists of things he disliked about both me and our marriage. I took these seriously and tried to discuss them with him. This got us absolutely nowhere. He wanted me to agree to new rules, which I was actually willing to consider—I was willing to walk through fire if that would bring us together again. But as soon as we would get specific about one of the rules, he would change it. He seemed to dislike me being cooperative and negotiable as much as he disliked me opposing his beliefs and wishes. I couldn't win.

In her book, *A Brilliant Madness* about her own manic-depressive illness, the actress Patty Duke writes: "Spouses blame themselves for not being able to turn the illness around, and often there is ambivalence about who is the failure: the one who is ill or the one who can't make him better."

I could not consistently stay solidly in contact with the fact that Jim was sick. I suppose that unconsciously I must have thought that if I accepted that fact, I would have to also accept my utter powerlessness to change what was happening. Accepting that Jim was so severely mentally ill also meant something pretty horrific about our future. That is, even if he were to heal and return to the Jim I knew, another manic episode would now always be lurking as a real possibility.

If Jim had died more simply—an auto wreck, cancer, a heart attack—I believe I would have been left feeling much stronger. The same is true if he had simply fallen into a depression without the year of mania. Over our nine good years, Jim's love for me had been so healing and had strengthened my self-esteem. But as he unraveled, he also unraveled my belief in myself as a loving, attractive, and deserving woman. He retracted that healing love and respect and said it had been a mistake. I was left not only with his no longer caring for me, but with the knowledge that this man who had really known me for nine years now said I was not worth it.

Still searching for answers several years after Jim died, I went to a talk at Princeton given by Kay Redfield Jamison. In the question-and-answer period at the end, I asked what a person could do when someone she cares for is in the midst of a manic episode. Dr. Jamison answered, "Ask the woman next to you—that's my mother." When the laughter subsided, Dr. Jamison stated simply, "Nothing. All you can do is take care of yourself."

9

GETTING HELP

I sought counseling during The Bad Year, but at the same time I had no patience for it. At various times in my life, I had seen a therapist, and it had sometimes been useful. But now all I really wanted was for Jim to change back. Putting *my* life in order held little interest for me.

Also, I believed that the pain I was going through was worse than any other pain there could be, and I didn't think that anyone could understand unless they had endured something similar. And perhaps I simply did not want to normalize the pain of my situation by thinking therapy could help.

It was probably a mistake to not stick with counseling. If I could have found the right therapist, it might well have helped me through the maze of my feelings. As Goodwin and Jamison say in *Manic-Depressive Illness*: "Mood disorders alter the perceptions and behaviors not only of those who have them but also those closely related."

Who would have been "the right therapist"? I would have wanted a therapist who spent part of each session helping me develop strategies for dealing with Jim's manic behaviors. It would have been a sign of understanding and support and would have fostered trust. Ordinarily in therapy, it is not considered good practice to spend much time talking about the problems of a third person; but in this case, there was so much difficult behavior to negotiate around, I needed basic help with strategy. Paradoxically, the therapist would have also been helping me to accept my powerlessness.

"The right therapist" would have encouraged me to fill my time to offset my obsessing. It would have been helpful to be told, "If you are determined to hang in, it is important to do things so that each day feels like more than just waiting for the mania to change, so that there is something to show for it."

The therapist would have given me facts about manic-depressive illness, specifically that however long it took, Jim would eventually cycle down from his mania.

Mostly what I would have wanted from a therapist was for someone to keep me aware of how I kept getting thrown off balance by how much I was personalizing and absorbing Jim's projections that I was the one with the problem. I think that this would have gone far in helping me keep my strength. It would have been useful to have been encouraged to read and reread descriptions of mania as well as my own journal writings over the course of Jim's manic episode. Mania is powerful, and it can take constant "inoculations" to help withstand it.

Early on I found a national organization, the Depression and Manic-Depression Association, DMDA (now renamed DBSA, Depression and Bipolar Support Alliance), which offers meetings on a local level. While visiting two therapist friends in Berkeley, California, in the early part of The Bad Year, I attended a meeting that turned out to be an oasis for me. The people seemed similar to me and Jim, and I fantasized us being able to attend such a group together once he was well. I imagined that these would be people who knew us, who could caution us, be mirrors for us, help us to prevent this horror from reoccurring.

There were subgroups for people who themselves were diagnosed with manic-depressive illness, others for family members and friends. I found it most helpful to talk with people who were diagnosed. To hear people speak of how out of control they were in their manic times and to hear them recommend hospitalization helped me to accept my viewing Jim as a mentally ill person and to feel less pain about it. One man framed it for me in a unique way—he said that I would need to do what women have done through the years when their men who went off to war were missing in action or prisoners of war: wait, live with the unknown, and pray for a safe return.

Everyone in the group thought Jim would crash sooner rather than later. Nothing anyone said helped me to prepare for the endurance test I was to withstand over the course of that year.

I was open about my sorrow and fear and received much support. By encouraging me with suggestions and strategies, these people who had deeply hurt the ones they loved during the times they had been manic had an opportunity to "do good," to use their experience to try to help me. It was a way for them to make amends of a sort, and we could cry together.

Some of what I heard at this meeting I referred back to throughout The Bad Year:

1. It is natural to try to get off medication, to follow the seduction of the mania.

2. On a manic high, nothing matters, not arrest, not money, not rules. It doesn't matter what I say. Nothing can touch "God." "It's like the marines on shore leave," one person said.

3. Let Jim be; he will cycle and burn out, probably only two more months.

4. He will probably not cycle to "normal," but will "crash and burn" in a deep depression. Or get arrested.

5. I do not recognize this Jim, manic. I will likely not recognize that Jim either, depressed.

6. I cannot control him.

7. Do what I can to protect myself so I can remain patient and not give up on him. Write him, do not call. Send him letters, a photo, so he has something of me when he plunges.

8. Eventually it will be me deciding whether I can stay with him. Jim will be clinging to me.

To my sorrow, the DMDA group in Nashville was not particularly helpful for me. However, the psychiatrist who was the consultant to this group was a former colleague of mine who had worked at the mental health center where I had been a social worker fifteen years before. His specialty was mood disorders. I called him.

Glen was enormously helpful throughout the months I was in Nashville. Never having met Jim, he advised me on the basis of his extensive experience with manic-depressive illness and my descriptions of Jim's behavior. Although I did not always take his advice, he continued to provide information and noncritical counsel.

Glen defined Jim as being in a "mixed state"—irritable, angry, aggressive, belligerent, and weeping and said that this is harder to treat. Amazingly, with medication, he could likely be stabilized in a week.

But Jim had been in a manic episode for a long time, and while Glen felt he was slowing and would settle down, he also felt that Texas was a low-stress environment and would present no ready crises. Glen thought that the confrontational letters I had asked friends to send Jim were a great way to try to stress him to produce a crisis.

Glen told me that I had no "muscle" on him, no leverage and that Jim's mixed state would get stickier and harder to treat.

"He needs intervention now," Glen said. "This illness gets worse with age, and Jim has had enough episodes to show he will need medication for maintenance forever."

Glen felt that lithium might not be the drug of choice since Jim had "breakthrough episodes" several times—the three short depressions and his previous manic episode. "Three mood swings and you're out" was Glen's policy.

"We hope for Jim to get depressed because then he will have insight, but not so depressed that he is suicidal." Glen felt that suicide was a big risk factor. I couldn't even imagine it.

"Or we hope he'll get belligerent enough to get in trouble." Glen said that Jim's use of marijuana was "like kerosene on a fire."

Glen stressed that Jim had a good track record for buying into the illness and accepting treatment and for being responsible with medications. "This is a good sign. But his long manic cycle is a real setup for a very long depression.

"A person who is manic only changes his mind when he is forced to. If you return to live with Jim, he'll see this as you agreeing with him. You have to be tougher than he is. Don't budge an inch. Don't negotiate at all. You will always lose. He is insatiable, and one demand will merely lead to another."

Glen advised me to write a letter to Jim in which I set firm limits using "tough love." He suggested something like "If you have any love for me, you will get treatment. There is no way I will live with you until you are stabilized on medicine. I am not able to tell you I love you anymore. Your mood will have to be stable before I can be with you or communicate anymore."

If, as a result, he filed for divorce, that's what happens. There was nothing I could do about it.

Yet Glen always added that I should not lose hope. "This illness has a great prognosis, if treated. Your position is to just wait. Someday he will be depressed. Then he will call you and say he needs you and is ashamed."

Glen's bottom line was that I should have no more

communication with Jim until he was willing to be in treatment.

When I asked Glen whether this was being unfair to Jim and should he not be allowed to choose what life he wanted, Glen replied, "Yes, if he wants to lose things. But this isn't his normal self. This self cannot choose well."

The consultations with Glen were a lifeline for me. Counsel that Glen gave felt like counsel Jim would have given me when he was healthy. I clung to his words, wanting reassurance that Jim would/could return to his former loving solid self. Glen's insights and opinions gave me something to hold on to.

Glen talked with me several more times even though I was not willing to stop all communication with Jim. Glen, of course, thought it was a bad idea for me to go to Texas each time I went. "Your heart will get hurt. Period." However, when I went anyway, he listened to my reports and responded.

Glen felt it important that everyone in Jim's life assume the same stance. "We love you, and you are acting insane. This is a product of your illness. We are aligning ourselves with your sanity. We are seeing you ruin and throw away what we know your sane self holds precious and dear."

He advised me to say, "Your lists and letters indicate that you are still way out of line. When you are stable, you will see the absurdity of this. I will save these papers so you can see how sick you can get."

And finally, Glen said, "Don't go near him, Judy. You would be living under his constant wrath."

All of this was such good advice and so generously

given, and yet I was unable to follow much of it. Call it loyalty, call it weakness—I was simply afraid to take steps that I thought might put at risk the hope I still held for the return of our formerly blissful life together.

As the year wore on and nothing changed, I somehow summoned the energy and vision to attempt to create a new structure for myself. Returning to school sounded comforting, and I learned of an exciting program in New York City. I had been a songwriter for many years and had cowritten several musicals, so I decided to apply to the Tisch School of the Arts at New York University, which offered a two-year master's of fine arts degree in musical theater writing.

It took every bit of my strength just to complete the application process, but I was accepted and was to begin in September 1997. After being adrift for many months, I finally had a plan for the future.

It was frightening to take steps that represented movement apart from Jim. I reassured myself that if things got better, Jim would probably welcome the chance to live in New York City for a while where he could study photography. And of course, I could always back out of the program if that seemed best. But at least I had something to fortify my identity separate from that as Jim's abandoned partner.

I also decided to learn to ride a motorcycle. I had always loved riding as a passenger, and something about the "tough girl" image appealed to my weakened self. I took a course with the Motorcycle Safety Foundation and then bought "Zoe," a 1981 Honda 250. Riding gave me great freedom and another new piece of identity. It also gave me a new community to which to belong. In that most hideous of years, I felt like an alien on an unfamiliar planet. I needed to belong somewhere.

10

PULLING APART

Jim began threatening divorce as soon as he left in August 1996. With my twenty-twenty hindsight, I am now pretty clear that Jim never wanted a divorce; he wanted us. But my desire for him to be back on lithium was intolerable to him and totally incompatible with his manic grandiosity.

Since there could be no discourse about lithium, tension over money was our major battleground that year. Although Jim had plenty of money available in his own accounts, he doggedly pressured me to separate our joint money. In an effort to keep him from draining all his resources, I refused. In every discussion about this, as with everything else, Jim was right, period. Where formerly we had been proud of our ability to discuss anything, always wanting the best for each other, neither of us blaming nor trying to win, now there was no negotiating with Jim. His only goal was to make me see that I was wrong.

The only way for Jim to get everything divided—our house, our belongings, our land in Washington—was through divorce. Finally, after many threats by Jim about getting an attorney, on May 5, 1997, I found divorce papers in my mailbox.

I did not want a divorce. Even though I had been living without Jim for many months by then, I did not want to consider life forever without him. But I had to face reality—the divorce papers were there in front of me.

After much weeping, I responded as was legally appropriate. I hired an attorney in Alpine to sort through the technicalities and to deal with Jim's interpretation of the law. Jim had a lot of ideas about what he was entitled to since he continued to believe that everything was my fault.

I was still hoping every minute that Jim would crash. At the same time, I was realizing that I was going to have to face a whole new nightmare, the division of our property.

This process was complicated. For one thing, my belongings were spread out, some in our casita in Texas where Jim planned to stay and some in our travel trailer that Jim had left behind in Washington State and which would also be his in our settlement. To retrieve these things, I would have to make two trips. It felt too soon to be making these trips; but by this time, I had already committed myself to school in New York City, and I knew I would not have time to deal with these things come September.

Another complication was that we disagreed about the extent of Jim's responsibility 1) for the ruin of our truck and 2) for all the expenses I had paid on our credit card for his trip around the country, hundreds of dollars of phone calls, thousands in gas, motels, restaurants. Jim saw these as joint expenses since he never thought of himself as having left me. His version of what happened was that I had not come along with him because I was going to Hawaii to help my brother move and then I had not come home to him in Texas because I had been depressed over my father's death. Jim could never see how savagely he had torn himself from our life—taking off his wedding ring, screaming at me as he drove away, leaving me stranded.

The essence of the complexity of dividing our property was that I was having to proceed with negotiations with a man who no longer negotiated. In his place was an ogre who was to be the executor of Jim's portion of our joint life, an uncaring arrogant ogre who could control important parts of my life.

Thankfully, we had lawyers to help keep things on target and to interpret the law to Jim, who believed that his interpretation was Truth. It was apparent to me, for example, that his eventual willingness to take some small responsibility for the death of our truck was the workings of his attorney, Frank; Jim would never in a million years have conceded that.

Throughout this process, I was still clinging to the hope that Jim's chemistry would change and I would be restored to his life and his love. But as the divorce progressed, even though I still wanted us to reunite, I also began wanting to disentangle everything, share nothing, own nothing together. I wanted to wind my life back onto its own spool. If the divorce signified an end to the waiting mode, then I needed to retrieve my self.

I have to admit that part of me wanted to fight Jim, to have my "day in court" in which to sing my own tragic opera of the previous year. (The same confusion that kept me uncertain about Jim's illness also interfered with my feeling much anger during The Bad Year. It probably would have strengthened me to recognize my anger more often.) However, I was advised that a court battle would end up costing me and be likely to provide little in return. I might not even have the satisfaction of a judge agreeing with my position, let alone any actual financial restitution, symbolic or otherwise.

Instead, I was encouraged to cut my losses and get out, to agree to things that sealed a bargain and did not represent too much of a violation and loss. The whole point was that everything was a violation and a loss. My life had been vandalized, and I was not insured.

There was clearly no way for this separation of property, this divorce, this tragedy to be fair. It just "was," and let's get done with it.

I planned the two trips to retrieve my belongings in quick succession. The easier one was to Washington State, so I made that trip first.

The timing of my trip turned out well. In a place where clouds and dampness usually prevailed, the sun was shining, and it was warm and dry at the beach; camping was easy. But being in Washington was sad. It was a return to the last place Jim and I had lived together, the scene of the demise of our relationship. It also represented the beginning of the disentangling of my life from Jim's and was a dress rehearsal for the more difficult trip to Texas.

For ten months, our travel trailer had been sitting in

an overgrown field, getting moldy. We had lived in that trailer for three years while building our casita, had slept in that bed night after night. Now there it was, moldy and abandoned, a reflection of how I had been feeling that whole year.

Jim had taken many things out of the trailer, but there was still a lot to deal with. I boxed what was mine, stuffed it into the rental car, and ultimately shipped it back to Nashville. One trip down, one to go.

The trip to Texas would be much harder for a variety of reasons. Foremost was that I would be seeing Jim for the first time in five months. The last time had been in Nashville in front of our old house as he laid rubber racing off in our truck, yelling, "Get your mind out of the gutter, Judy Eron!" I was full of dread about seeing him in Texas, afraid of what awfulness this encounter would unleash. I was worried that his anxiety and my anxiety would collide, and he would do some version of what had occurred previously, such as a) punching the Jeep window, screaming; or b) locking me out of the house, screaming; or c) screeching off in his vehicle, screaming.

There was also the finality—this would be it, no more life together. It felt like I was losing us all over again. Somehow, having my clothes and his still hanging in the same closet helped to protect my hope of a reunion.

Lastly the trip to Texas would be hard because I would be going to the house that had been our dream, the house Jim and I had built with love and sweat and great determination. It was Heartbreak City I was going to, and I had no choice but to go there.

I was fortunate to have my friend Marge with me for this treacherous trip. Marge and I had been friends for more than twenty years. She had helped me do a similar unraveling of another household when my mother died in 1982 and we moved my father from our family home to an apartment. Marge had been perfect for the task of helping me sift through my mother's belongings, clothes, perfumes, making the difficult decisions of what to keep and what to give away. Now Marge was going to help me close up another portion of my life, do another seemingly impossible task.

When we arrived in Alpine to pick up the moving truck, I stopped in to talk with my attorney who informed me that he and I had a meeting scheduled that morning with Jim and his lawyer to try to come to final decisions. This took me by surprise, but I had to do it.

When I entered the room, Jim was already seated, unshaven and in rumpled clothes. Instinctively I went to him and kissed him. He was receptive for about one nanosecond.

The meeting did not go well. The disagreement was mostly over the value of our truck that had died. This was Bernice, our 1993 3\4 ton, 4x4, Cummins Diesel, extended-cab Dodge truck, the truck we had thoroughly researched and then delightedly shopped for in preparation for our Getaway, the truck which had been such an integral part of our Getaway life itself.

I had been in charge of maintaining our vehicles, and at the beginning of the summer of 1996, at three-and-a-half-years old and with 90,000 miles on her, Bernice was in great shape. However, between the time that Jim left me in late August, and around March when

Bernice died, he had put an additional 60,000 miles on her. When we lived together at our casita, Jim and I usually went out the eighteen miles of dirt road once a week, at most. Jim living alone in his expansive state of mind would go in and out at least once each day. Also, he drove the dirt road fast, putting a lot of stress on the truck body, and this ended up bending the frame.

In March, I heard through the Texas grapevine, and later from Jim, that Bernice was defunct. "I was just driving back from the store, Judy, when something happened, and the engine overheated and froze. It turned out that Bernice had no water in her." I was furious, but kept it to myself. And so our $26,000 truck bit the dust at only four years old. Jim traded Bernice for a 1981 truck whose value was around $2,000.

In this meeting with the attorneys, Jim was insisting that he was not responsible for Bernice's demise. I was also insistent, but Jim kept interrupting. Jim's lawyer, Frank, told me after Jim's death that he had never seen this side of Jim—so out of control and rude. Later, too, Frank understood why I had been so insistent about the truck, that its demise was a metaphor for the mess that Jim's illness had made of our entire relationship, a tangible representation of the scrap heap of our marriage.

When we left that meeting, Jim was completely unapproachable. The plan had been for us to divide our joint possessions at the casita. But now Jim no longer wanted Marge and me to stay at the house and was no longer willing to go through the process of dividing our things.

"I don't know if I want to trust you being there,

Judy, taking things."

"Jim, I came all this way to get my things. You agreed to do this."

"OKAY. I'll be there at the end of the day."

I was badly shaken by this meeting and didn't know if this whole project of retrieving my belongings might now be sabotaged. Marge and I drove to the house and got to work at dismantling and packing. Marge was very efficient, and by the time Jim arrived, a lot had been done. We left the boxes open so that Jim could examine everything if he wanted.

Jim arrived about 6 P.M. and took a look at the chaos. Understandably upset by the upheaval, he stomped off to the patio to sit and smoke. I went out and asked him if he was ready to go through things.

"What do you want, Judith? What is it you want?"

"I want to sort through our belongings and divide them, Jim, like we agreed we would do when I got here."

"I'm not going to do that."

"Well, what are you doing here?"

"Judith, what is it you're doing? That with the lawyers is a travesty of justice. What are you doing?"

He spat out more accusations, belligerent and mean. I walked away and went back to packing. I was angry, confused, and miserable. I was abhorred by my own dearest love.

After a while, I went back out. Jim started to badger me again.

"What do you want, Judith Eron? Aren't you concerned at all with forgiveness? When are you going to talk about forgiveness, Judith?"

I was aware that Marge was being subjected to this

harangue and suggested to Jim that he and I take a walk. Amazingly, he agreed.

The walk that Jim and I took turned out to be transforming, and he credited me with that in the weeks to come. We walked a familiar path from our house down our dirt road. This was a walk we had taken every evening for the three years that we had lived in our travel trailer at the casita, building our home. It was a short walk, perhaps a quarter of a mile each way.

When we would take this walk in the evenings, we would head away from the house and at the end of the road, we would turn around and look back at our progress in the construction of the house, marveling at our accomplishment. It was a time when we could actually "ooh and ah" over ourselves. Then we would head back home to clean up from dinner, with Jim washing dishes and me reading to him. Those were precious times.

Now as we walked, Jim asked me, "Judy, when are you going to forgive?"

I felt confused by this question. Who was he asking me to forgive? Jim had never apologized or taken any responsibility for his behavior the past year, his destruction of our life together. This was the first time I had heard him talk about forgiveness in that direction. In my confusion and self-blame all year, I often felt it was only I who needed to be forgiven, that I had let Jim down and been a bad wife, that I was solely to blame just as he kept saying I was.

"Jim, I don't know what to say. I'm not really thinking about me forgiving you. I want *you* to forgive *me*."

Jim was not expecting that reversal, and I think the

surprise of it, although unintended, changed his mind-set. His belligerence disappeared, his anger evaporated.

"Jim, I'm so very sorry that I couldn't be a better friend to you this year. I knew you were scared last summer, and I wasn't there for you. My own fear got in the way, and I feel terrible about that. I feel terrible for letting you down, for doing anything to lead you to think that I wasn't on your side. You are my most beloved person, and I let you down."

By this time, I was weeping. I stopped walking, turned toward him, took his hands in mine, and said, "I am so, so sorry, Jim. Please forgive me."

Somewhere in there Jim started weeping, too, and he held me, and we sobbed together. I kept repeating, "I'm so sorry, I'm so sorry." And Jim kept saying, "I know. I know." We stood there weeping together, holding one another.

During the more than ten months since this horrible nightmare had begun, I had told Jim more than once that I felt responsible for part of our mess, that I was willing to work on myself and our relationship. Some of this admission had come from my confusion about his illness and some from my willingness to do anything to bring us back together. Apologizing was not new behavior for me; but something was different about this moment in July, a tenderness, perhaps, that released something in him.

I can't say how much of his receptiveness was due to my being so undefended with him and how much was due to the changes in his own brain chemistry. In our good years, Jim had always been touched by my willingness to be vulnerable with him, what he called "exposing your neck in a fight." Whatever it was, Jim softened and began to acknowledge and apologize for the first time in more than a year.

"I left you, Judy. I did. I left you," he admitted tearfully.

So much was said on that walk, and as I listened, I basked in Jim's apology and willingness to be close to me again. He was completely different from just minutes before.

"I'll go down on my knees for your forgiveness for all I did to you," he said. "When we met, I told you I was fucked up—and here it is. I've been so deeply threatened by your interactions with others. But I couldn't express my fear or my anger.

"Judy, maybe we had too much. So close by in Mexico, there's such poverty, and we had so much. So much love, such a comfortable life.

"Judy, I got different. Call it bipolar, call it chemicals, call it God. I got different."

Another thing that Jim talked about was his family. He asked me for help regarding them. "What should I do? How shall I proceed to get things right with them?"

I suggested he do with them like he was doing with me that very evening, taking his share of the responsibility. He shook his head and said, "No. I want an accounting from them of their behavior."

I took a risk and let my guard down. "Jim, my experience is that when I give you an accounting, you don't like the accounting and you get angry and forceful and overbearing." To my surprise, Jim said, "You're right."

It was amazing to be having an actual back-and-forth conversation with Jim for the first time in a year. I felt no fear or anger. However slightly, something about this visit was prying open a deadbolted door.

One important thing that Jim said to me that evening he had said at various times throughout The Bad Year: "If I resolve things with you, Judy, I'm scared what will happen to me. I get such power from my anger and righteousness." In light of what eventually happened, this statement takes on a particularly eerie aspect.

As we sat and looked at the mountains, a storm came up rather suddenly, with thunder and huge clouds. When it began to pour, we ran for shelter in the shed across the driveway from the house. We sat on the dirt floor and laughed and held each other, continuing to talk and feel close.

When it rains at the casita, the dirt road turns to a type of clay similar to what potters use, becoming sticky and dangerous for driving. So, of all things, Jim had to spend the night. Marge and I were sleeping in the house; Jim slept alone in the camper. He later told me that he had hoped it would rain for days and I would not be able to leave, but would have to stay there at the casita, close to him.

Before bed, Marge and Jim and I had supper together. Marge was deeply touched and sad for him. Marge does not cry often; yet when she and I were alone, she wept again and again. She felt very sad that Jim was losing me and that he could not really see how sick he was. She was surprised by her own feelings and her openness to Jim. She had come to the casita with some fear of what he might do. In fact, she told me later that when we arrived, she had seen his shotgun and hidden it "just to be safe." But being with him, she could see how lost he was.

I returned to Nashville hoping that there would remain some of the closeness Jim and I had just felt, something we could build upon. I was hoping he might start to call, but he didn't. When I called him and asked if he missed me, he replied, "No, I don't miss you. But I do see the reason I've been in a relationship with you. It's real apparent to me, and it is very present. I feel proud of you, Judy." He was so able to compartmentalize his feelings.

Several days after my return to Nashville, my forty-ninth birthday passed sadly with no call or card from Jim. Shortly after, I took a trip to be with family in upstate New York for my aunt's eighty-fifth birthday and then went to see my new apartment in New York City for the first time. (My cousins had selected it for me.) I stayed in New Jersey with my other aunt while my uncle was in the hospital. I was away from Nashville from July 25 to August 1. The dates become important in this countdown to Jim's change of heart and change of chemistry and ultimately to his death. Returning to Nashville on August 1, I had only twelve days until Jim called to reclaim me as his partner. I also had only two months and ten days left of Jim on this earth.

I had counted on the trip to Texas helping me with my sense of separation from Jim. Instead, it felt like another false alarm in which I believed that change might be happening, followed by another disappointment. In my journal, I wrote of weeping day after day, not being able to adjust to life without Jim, yet knowing that school in New York City, just weeks away, was the structure I had chosen to hold me while I tried to go on. I rode my motorcycle, wrote, played music with my friend, Pablo, and I spent time with friends and family members. But I felt as awful as I had at any time during that terrible year.

11

FINALLY

What happened next defies ordinary interpretations. Even now, I cannot fit the sequence of events that occurred into any logic. What happened seemed almost miraculous, at least for a while.

It is also true that as it turned out, with Jim's suicide, I sometimes look at those next two months as the universe having teased me, even tortured me—bringing Jim back to me and then killing us both with one bullet. However, in my more open-minded and grateful moments, I see that time as God or the universe saying, "I can't bring Jim back to you forever. The best I can do is to give him to you briefly and lead him to apologize to you so you know you weren't crazy all along and so you know how he loved you."

In any case, this is how it unfolded, the final rise and fall on our sixteen-month roller-coaster ride.

As mentioned, I returned to Nashville from New York on August 1 to prepare for my move to New York City at the end of the month. Those next days in my journal are full of anguished statements: "Wedding rings piss me off, sadden me." "I hate being in this life." "Oh, God, I miss my Jim."

Nothing about how I felt had improved, despite having completed the difficult trips to Washington State and Texas, despite having retrieved my belongings, despite knowing that I would be moving to New York to start school in a few weeks. Every day was still hell.

Meanwhile, Jim attended a family reunion in Wisconsin the first week in August. His family's response to him further confused and saddened me. Roy said, "If you didn't know who he was before, he'd seem pretty normal." Jim's parents were just happy to see him. Jim's sister, however, said Jim was very quiet, and did not seem normal to her. "He has no sensitivity, no warmth, no integrity. He has a different personality and a different soul now."

I was continuing to accuse myself, as I had done many times during The Bad Year, of doing the wrong things all year. And I was completely exhausted from all the emotions of the past weeks.

It was in this shaken, depleted, self-blaming state that I received Jim's phone call on Monday, August 11. He was calling to say that CBS News was coming to the casita the next day to interview him about his work on the air pollution problem with Clean Air for Big Bend. He sounded so okay to me, which only further upset me.

When the phone call ended, I sat there once again contrasting how great Jim's life seemed at that moment with what a mess I felt I was. I could not hold on to the fact that although this might seem true, it was also true that Jim's successes were being fueled by his mental illness.

I needed to take some action; I was driving myself crazy with these feelings and thoughts. It became suddenly clear to me that I needed to fully confront myself with the fact of Jim's mental illness, to find some way to look at clear evidence.

I had a perfect way to do this, something I had been meaning to do for a long, long time. Jim's actions due to his mental illness had been headline news in 1982. I went to the public library to look up the newspaper articles about his disappearance from both his family and the army that year, when he had first been diagnosed with manic-depressive illness, a little more than four years before I had met him.

This was a formidable thing for me to do. I didn't know what I would find or how I would react. I felt like I was in someone's short story; it was surreal sitting there in a row of people at microfilm machines reading about my husband's insanity. If they only knew the bizarre quest I was on.

The articles were surprisingly easy to find. I found five in all, the first dated November 22, 1982, in which Jim was reported as missing from his family and AWOL from the army. The last article was dated January 11, 1983, when he was found and sent to a military hospital in Atlanta, Georgia. These articles were eyeopening, to put it mildly. Twice, Jim had even been front-page news. Here are the headlines from the *Nashville Tennessean*:

- November 22, 1982: "Psychologist Missing; Officials Fear Foul Play"
- November 24, 1982: "Missing Man's Car Found Here"
- November 26, 1982: "Police, Army: Opinions Conflict In Psychologist Hunt" (front page)
- January 9, 1983: "AWOL Doctor Snared In Shoplifting Arrest" (front page)
- January 11, 1983: "Army Psychologist Moved For Testing"

Reading these articles was mind boggling. It was hard to take in that this was my beloved Jim, the man I had selected as my husband. I had known the story, but there was something about seeing it in print that made the reality clearer and more alarming. And of course, I had not known when I began loving Jim just how repeatable it could be.

In those moments of reading the articles, I wished with all my heart that Jim and I had read them together early in our relationship. As I had thought many times during The Bad Year, and have thought many times since, perhaps we would have taken Jim's illness more seriously if we had equipped ourselves with more information. I might not have become so entangled in his perspective had I known more. I did not have the vantage that I have now.

I left the library with a head full, just what I had come for. I had copies of the articles, palpable in my hand.

It is a sad statement about my sorry state that

despite this, I called both Paul and Marge that night, needing for the thousandth time to be told that Jim's behavior change was due to mental illness, not me. Even having seen all that information in black and white, still I had trouble holding on to the fact that Jim was sick. He had sounded so grounded that morning. In fact, at around 10:30 P.M., right before I went to sleep, I wrote in my journal: "How can he be so okay?"

At 11:45 P.M., the phone rang, waking me. It was Jim, but a different Jim than fifteen hours earlier. This Jim was talking a mile a minute, his thinking paranoid and jumbled. As I had done all year when I spoke with him, I took notes in my journal as he spoke. Consequently, this transcription is pretty accurate.

Jim had much to talk about, and he did so with very few stops.

"Judy, CBS News will be here at 9 A.M. And this is megastuff, Judy. Because Dan Rather is from Texas. And the marines shot and killed an eighteen-year-old boy who was herding goats in Redford. And I talked with people, and some of them want it and some don't, more border protection.

"Do you know a law has been passed and seriously, tonight I talked to my son and I talked to the head of Big Bend National Park. They might do something on the border, put up like the Sinai, a barrier. It's seriously being discussed by serious people, Judy. It has people going."

Here, he started to cry, and I tried to soothe him. "I'm here, Jim. Take your time."

Jim took awhile, then went on. "You look good, Judy." (Referring to seeing me the month before when I had come to Texas for my things.) "It should be factored in. And I will listen to your music. I'm not needing to be as alienated from our prior state. I've not been out of love with you, Judy." Then, "We owe so much to Marge, for making that time so peaceful. Judy, your honesty was deeply felt. It's a great story. You must know you're in high regard here at the ranch. Seriously.

"Judy, things are happening here in a funny way. Just watch. Let's work toward closure. We'll finish our stuff.

"At the family reunion in Milwaukee, everybody behaved. I was quiet. My son was there, which was fortunate, he's very neat. If you want to take on a megaresponsibility, take my mother to his graduation.

"Judy, when we get our money clear, if you want to, we can meet and go see him. I want you to know I'm not prickly, but I'm not here throwing anything off to tease you. This year will come together. I'm still feeling.

"Minna is not an entanglement. [Minna is a woman Jim told me he had been involved with on the ranch.] Oh, and here's some news. That woman down the road from us is leaving her new husband. Call her, Judy. No, don't.

"All this acceleration. Everything else gets electric because of those stupid New York people. Serious politics. I've been involved with more educated people in less personal ways—the attorney Mary Kelly."

I said, "You're doing good work, Jim."

"Well, Judy Eron, where did my energy go? Into this project. I'm still taking pictures. I send my rolls to Portland to develop. I had good contact. That music festival. Judy, Milwaukee's a fan of yours, of your music. I want a tape of you and Pablo. I gave you that photo of your father, and I wasn't going to.

"The reunion—my brother got seventy-five people to come there. But seriously, it's good about the big bonus of this whole thing. Judy, you are regarded by everyone. Hey, you didn't say anything about the photo I sent you of the baby. But thanks for the note about me being a grandfather."

I said, "Jim, I hold myself back. I could pour and pour all over you."

"Minna has total regard for you, Judy. I've tried to explain it nineteen different ways, and she still says, 'Now what did Judy do wrong?' She spoils her kids, Judy. And there's no sex thing. Minna is very helpful about business and has good friends."

I said, "Jim, you called because you were feeling anxious?"

"Yeah. I wanted to blab. I appreciate your being receptive. I thought you would be. I may stay up all night. My sleep has been good. But I still watch it."

"Jim, people care about you?"

"Yes. How about you, Judy? You're well friended."

"Yes."

"With boys? What do you do with boys, Judy?"

"I ride motorcycles with boys."

"Is that all?"

"You don't want to hear."

"Yes I do . . . No, I don't."

"Jim, it's nice to know I'm special to you."

"Good. Judy, we'll finish our transaction. You can come here. Tell me what you need. I'll burn the fucking house down if it's keeping you away."

"Jim, I don't know what to say to you. I love you,

Jim, but I won't tell you stuff. I know you don't want to hear it."

"That's right. This call was me reaching out to you. We followed through. We get kudos, Judy, we finished the house, where others haven't done that. I don't need much analyzing. I have gobs of friends. I have very little need to do analysis these days. I'm okay. But I can get wired.

"Judy, that music by Vangelis was the high point of our relationship. On the mountain at Lake Powell."

"I know, Jim. But I can't listen to it now. I weep a lot. I feel differently from you."

"I'm indebted, Judy. I'll get off now. This will cost a million dollars." He hung up.

And so the phone conversation ended. It was 12:37 A.M. What I mostly felt was "my poor baby." His mind was speeding, so upset. At first I thought there was going to be a point, a reason why he had called, something bad, like the house had burned down. He was that intense and pressured. But after a while, I realized that there was no point. Jim was just awake and anxious and feeling "us." And he trusted that I would hold him over the phone.

I could understand from the call that Jim loved me and wanted me. I knew that he also wanted his high. Yet I could feel that he was uncomfortable, and I felt a glimmer of the possibility that he could get back to his normal self again, which I had begun to seriously doubt could happen even if he were back on medication. This interaction made me feel that he was retrievable.

Coming just hours after my reading the articles about

Jim's illness, the call felt to me like a message from the universe, saying, "Hang on, Judy. It will happen. Jim will be back with you, healed, medicated." But also cautioning me, "This is Jim, and he is not well. Read the articles. Look. Listen. See. Hear. He is ill, and you need to accept that. He is not a partner the way he is."

I wrote in my journal at 2 A.M., after the call, "A second chance, God? Am I a fool? Or am I your angel, to help bring Jim back?"

I felt excited, hopeful. Yet deep down, I had the feeling that tomorrow this call would likely be nothing to Jim, just another false alarm. I simply had to keep my feet grounded and continue to saturate myself even more with the facts of Jim's illness.

The next day was Tuesday, August 12. Although still amazed at the call from Jim, I continued my quest, determined to call everyone I knew of who'd had dealings with Jim in the past when he had been in the grips of his illness. My goal was to hear people speak of Jim's illness, to press it into my brain that Jim was a different person when he was sick, to underscore for myself that his behavior within his illness was not a personal statement about me.

My first call was to a woman Jim had a relationship with near the end of his first marriage. She had been a sweet, though brief part of Jim's life, and he had told me much about their relationship. Jim had been candid about how she had become a victim of his mania that developed in the spring of 1985. Jim had never spoken to her since. He knew he had frightened her with his delusions and impaired judgment, and he did not want to impose himself on her in any way. I imagine, too, that he was ashamed.

I had never spoken with her before, and I was not sure how she would take my call. In fact, she was quite understanding of my need to talk with her and willing to tell me what she could. She knew that something was wrong with Jim again because he had called her on his trip through Nashville that past September, wanting to see her. Jim had told me this sometime in the previous months, saying only that she had been nice, but unwilling to meet with him.

Her version was a lot more charged than that. She told me that Jim's call had frightened her. It was clear that something was wrong with him again, that he was accelerating and was obviously manic. She worried that he might resume his pursuit of her and had cut things off before anything more could develop.

I told her about the year and that I was having a very difficult time coming to any closure or peace. I told her about our nine wonderful years and that I still deeply loved Jim and simply was not able to stop hoping or wanting him back.

I explained, "I'm calling you in an effort to flood myself with information about Jim's sickness, to try to convince myself that his mental illness is the root of all this mess, not my behavior as his wife. I am so lost in my response to his craziness. I'm desperate for help."

"Judy, I'll do what I can to help you. What do you want me to talk about?"

I told her that it would be helpful to hear her description of him as a manic person. This was not easy for her as it stirred up a lot of horrible memories. "Judy, our relationship was meaningful, but brief and complicated. It was frightening back then, and I am still afraid of him. He's so bright and so capable and so crazy and manipulative and power wielding. It amazes me that he's been able to 'circle the airport' as long as he has.

"He was very volatile then and put my family in a terrible position. He drove down to the small town I'm from and went to see my parents, toward what end I don't know—maybe to try to explain what our relationship had been. It was horrible. He was stalking me, and he was also obsessed with my baby daughter. I worried that he might try to kidnap her.

"Knowing him changed my life in some good ways, but it also almost destroyed my life, and me, too. He has such an obsessive quality to him, and I have a real fear of having him back in my life. I don't trust him.

"Jim was so wonderful that people responded in ways that fed his power-tripping and his fragile ego. He'd only been stable for about a year and a half before I met him, after his 'psychic fugue' when he disappeared. He was grandiose and always so good at finessing. I only really knew him for six months, and even in that time, the change was so rapid. He had started smoking marijuana again, and I just assumed he had stopped lithium." (I told her that he had not stopped lithium, that his mania in 1985 had been a "breakthrough manic episode," confirmed by blood tests at the time.)

She said, "It's amazing, the power of knowing someone like that and seeing the mental illness do what it did to him. I was afraid that things would not go well for him in the long haul."

How right she was.

She was clearly a rational and caring person. This conversation, especially hearing how wary of him she was, helped me. It clashed with my longing for Jim and my wish to resume my life with him, even at all costs. I admired her position that she would not allow Jim to hurt her further.

My next contact was two hours later when I went to the office of the pharmacist who had led the group for men with manic-depressive illness at the V.A. Hospital in Nashville. Jim had attended this group for seven years and had a lot of respect for the leader.

I arrived at his office unannounced. Once I told him what was happening, he had much to say. I was surprised, but grateful that he would talk with me so openly.

"Jim is so intelligent and quick," he said, "and he's determined to do this his own way. He'll never voluntarily get on a mood stabilizer. If he did get on medication, he'd easily clear up and become your old Jim. However, it's probably also true that both marijuana and manic-depressive illness have killed some of his brain cells.

"The fact that Jim is taking herbs to help him sleep and only wants 'natural' things in his body—well, lithium is the most natural—it's a body salt. He just needs more of it than most of us."

This man clearly liked and respected Jim, but also obviously understood what mania could do to him.

My next call was to the priest who had hired Jim in 1984 as psychologist for the Catholic diocese in Nashville. That was after Jim's hospitalization following his disappearance, and Jim had been grateful for the chance to work in his profession again. However, when Jim became manic in 1985 and had gone to this same priest for help, he had been disappointed in what he regarded as the priest's lack of understanding.

The priest was not enthusiastic about talking with me, but said, "I don't pretend to know about this illness, but I do know that you're not to blame. I myself went through that impulse to self-blame. After I took a risk and hired Jim within a year of his breakdown, I started to blame myself. He began to change and had no insight at all into his behavior.

"When Jim was in bad shape, he frightened me. He called me in the middle of the night. He had to see me. It was months since I'd last seen him, and he was crazy and incoherent. And he could not see this at all.

"Judy, Jim is not willing to do what it takes to stay okay. It's beyond his control, and you are just not part of this. You married him with good reason and tried to help him. He is a very talented and good man—he proved that. But he also proved that he is a very sick man and will probably stay that way. He can't seem to help destroying things in his life."

He ended saying, "God bless you."

I had more calls to make, but I'd had enough for one day.

That evening, Jim called to say, "Bridget Foley from CBS News came this morning in a ruby red Cadillac with two guys, and they filmed about the Clean Air for Big Bend project for hours." Jim was calmer, but still pressured.

"I said on camera, 'my wife Judy,' and then off camera, I told Bridget what happened between us."

I told him sincerely, "Good for you, Jim."

"Yes, Judy. Good for me. I knew you'd be interested. So take care. Bye."

I could feel the difference in myself, talking to him. I was fortified with the conversations and newspaper articles, and I actually did have more distance and perspective. At the same time, I felt my sadness keenly. I wrote in my journal: "The tragedy of this is even more apparent to me now." And I also wrote: "What considerable expertise I have at dismissing everything and anything that is a warning sign. Those newspaper articles about Jim blew my mind."

The next morning, I was at it again. This time I called the psychiatrist with whom Jim was working at Fort Campbell, Kentucky, in 1982, at the time of his disappearance. That psychotic depression had culminated in Jim's being hospitalized for several months at an army facility in Georgia where he was finally correctly diagnosed and put on lithium.

This doctor said that he understood my question about why, as a therapist, if I could help other people, why couldn't I do the same for Jim. He said that he had felt the same way.

"Judy, I was no use to Jim at all. I didn't see it coming—I marveled at all he was doing. I was excited about a project that Jim was working on and could only admire how he could do it all. And then he disappeared."

He went on to tell me that he and his wife had tried to take care of Jim's family when Jim disappeared. They bought bicycles for the boys at Christmas and led them to believe that somehow Jim had provided these gifts.

Over the years, Jim had spoken fondly and appreciatively to me about this man, acknowledging that he had been responsible for Jim's leaving the army with a medical disability instead of a dishonorable discharge. However, in our conversation, this psychiatrist said that Jim never acknowledged this to him, never expressed any appreciation. "In fact, Jim harbored a deep resentment toward me and toward medicine, that those in the medical profession just want to control people. That should be a clue, Judy. When Jim is not doing well, he has to distance from anyone he owes anything to or feels close to.

"The culprit isn't you, Judy. It's Jim's neurotransmitter system. Like a drug, once it gets hold of him, all insight is stolen from him."

I asked him about Jim's perspective that "this is the real me." His reply was that this was rationalization. "Judy, if there's anything a person can do to be a better person, one should do it. And Jim is not. He's so bright, it's easy for him to come up with this thing, 'the real me.' Stay out of that. He is just inflated and trying to rationalize being off medication."

Toward the end of our conversation, I asked him what Jim had been like when he was finally picked up by the police after nearly two months of wandering on the streets of Nashville, sleeping in doorways, and hanging out at the Greyhound bus station.

"It was actually quite anticlimactic. He was disheveled, unkempt, desperately depressed. He looked like a complete bum. There wasn't much interesting about him. It was an enormous anticlimax given the amount of publicity that had followed him. There was a lot of anger toward him from others, but he was such a lump—who could be angry?

"I only saw him once after that, I think. I ran into him in Nashville. That's when he said those cutting remarks about psychiatrists and medication."

That phone conversation clinched something for me. I finally began to digest that this whole thing was not about me. I was making progress in my search for something that would help me to let go of Jim.

And then the phone rang.

12

REUNION

Wednesday, August 13, 1997.

When I think back to this phone call, it is a shining pearl of a moment in a dreadfully dark year, especially when considered within the context of Jim's subsequent suicide. If he had died with us still so separate, the aftermath would probably have been even more difficult for me.

It all began with Jim's phone call, which came just minutes after my phone conversation with the psychiatrist.

"Judy, can you handle a bizarre phone conversation? Can you come down here to help me? As soon as possible? Minna dropped out, and I have this party for the air pollution thing on September 3, and Mary Kelly, the attorney, is coming from Austin, and I have to do it myself. I'm feeling overwhelmed, and so I asked some friends, and they said, 'Call Judy. She'll help you.' So here I am calling you, Judy, for help."

Jim was fast and choppy in his thinking and his topics: Who would be coming to the party on September 3, the ruby red Cadillac, fund-raising, CBS News, slide projectors he'd bought for the party, etc.

"Judy, a lot of details get complicated. Plus even more if you're feeling wired up from CBS News. It has nothing to do with me, you, or my individual pathology. This is mega, Judy.

"I'm asking you to come help me. I know I can trust you. I'm not begging or demanding. But that's where my mind goes, and you should know that. We both want to be together now, and that's the joke."

I was bowled over. I was weeping. Here was the full expression of my daily prayer, the hope I had held in my heart constantly for almost a year. But I was also afraid and wanted to make sure I knew what he was asking me to do. He had asked me to come to Texas twice before, and both times ended horribly.

"Jim, if I come, I'm coming as your wife. I would be coming to love you."

"Yes, Judy, that's what I want. I want to hold you and love you. If I can't handle your love, then I need a therapist. This is not a retreat, Judy, this is moving toward you. You don't have to worry. I guarantee your emotional safety. I won't lock myself in the darkroom." (He was referring to my visit in January when he had locked me out of the house and then locked himself in his darkroom.)

I wept some more. It was such a relief to be hearing him want me after so long.

"It's good, Judy. Given all the horrors, there's much to weep about and to not weep about."

"I want to come. Let me just think about it and call you right back."

"That's good, Judy. This is a phone call from God. Now it's between you and God."

We hung up. I was in ecstasy. Shock and ecstasy.

I wondered whether it would be "enabling" Jim if I went, helping him to reduce the anxiety that was enveloping him and pushing him to the edge? We all wanted Jim to go "over the edge" so he would be willing to get back on medication. On the other hand, I also wondered whether Jim was close to needing hospitalization and my going would put me there when it happened.

My friends were supportive of my going, given my more objective perspective of the last two days. They were also afraid for me, given Jim's volatility and viciousness during my previous visits. But no one criticized my need or desire to go.

I quickly called the airlines and booked myself on a flight the very next morning.

I called Jim back. "I have a flight out tomorrow, Jim, and I arrive at noon in Odessa."

"Wow. Great, Judy. Hey, listen, my car is messed up, so go ahead and rent a car, and I'll pay for it. In fact, I'll call and rent it and call you back. Or wait until you get to Dallas, and I'll tell you if I can meet you." He sounded so happy and excited.

To put this in a time perspective, this was Wednesday. Monday and Tuesday had been the days I had done my investigative work. I was to be leaving for school in two weeks, on Thursday, August 28, with a send-off party for me given by my Nashville friends on Thursday, August 21. This was literally the last window of time in which I could just pick up and go when Jim asked. The timing of that is still amazing to me.

And, of course, I went.

Between Monday night when he had called me before CBS News came and Thursday when I arrived at his side, Jim made a barrage of phone calls, much as he had done earlier in this nightmare. He called his mother, his son, Roy, my brother, and several of our friends. He also called some of the men in his men's group, who became very worried about him, his disjointed thoughts and fast-paced speech, and wondered whether they should call me. He kept this up, calling people to tell them that I was coming and that he meant it to be peaceful. He also called many people on the ranch to say that I was coming. He was feeling so full, so glad that I would be with him. I think that my agreeing to come validated him as still "okay," the "Judy stamp of approval," so to speak, as though he thought, "If Judy thinks I'm okay, then I'm okay."

This was a dream come true, not that I thought everything would be fine and we'd be married happily ever after again. Our divorce was still in progress, but I was relieved and overjoyed to be given the opportunity to be Jim's ally and act lovingly toward him. I was so happy finally flying down to Texas. Suddenly, instead of every minute being another minute of hell, every minute was bliss. It was bliss to finally be able to look forward to something.

I have to say that despite all the roller-coaster rides of that entire year, on this particular trip, I never once worried that Jim would change his request or his position. I believe this had to do with a new strength I was feeling as a result of those two days of immersing myself in Jim's illness. For the first time in a year, I was able to clearly see that Jim was sick and needed my help and that my need to have him back as the Jim I knew was secondary.

As I was changing planes in the Dallas airport, I called Jim to see whether he would be meeting me at the airport in Odessa or whether I should rent a car. He said to rent a car, and then he read a long list of items for me to purchase. The reality of his loose thinking and his lack of emotional connectedness hit me.

"Oh, good deal, Judy. Things have changed. It's okay. For the better. Mary Kelly called, and now it's a town meeting and not a party and not in September. So it's bigger, but I'm not responsible. So come to the Longhorn [a restaurant/meeting space]—I'll meet you there. Are you ready to work?"

My plane was boarding, and I needed to hurry him through his grocery list. I could feel myself getting anxious. I needed to contain my anxiety so it would not collide with Jim's anxiety and manic energy.

"Take your time, Judy. Come in good spirits. And when we're done working, you and I will drive in your rental car to the casita. Alone."

What work was it we were going to do at the Longhorn? Jim was on full speed; I wondered whether the "party" had been taken out of his hands. Perhaps people were finally seeing his impairment. (This turned out to be exactly the case.) When Jim told me that people were delighted I was coming, I wondered how much of their delight was based on a hope that I would know what to do for Jim.

As I drove to the Longhorn, I urged myself toward vigilance on several fronts: 1) It was a given that Jim's thinking was weird. I did not need to respond in ways that would emphasize this. Just accept it. 2) It was a given that Jim was smoking and would smell of cigarettes. Let it not be a big deal. 3) Jim talked excessively. Roll with it. 4) I needed to be in no hurry at any time. Always leave plenty of time and then some, so that no added anxiety would come from being in a rush.

I also had certain fantasies: 1) Jim would be wearing his wedding ring. 2) Jim would want me to take him to a doctor or to the V.A. 3) Jim would want to return to Nashville with me (this one came true). 4) To a person, everyone would want to help get Jim into the hospital. 5) Jim would have already started taking lithium again.

My best friend cautioned me that this "adventure" might turn out to be a wreck. But I believed it could also be the beginning of a miracle.

As I drove in the rental car, I listened to a tape of the Buddhist philosopher, Ram Dass, that Jim had sent me some time earlier. In it, he says that a social worker helping someone who isn't helped needs to think: You do what you do as part of a process. Therefore, don't be attached to the fruit of your actions. You do your best, and what happens happens. You do what you can do and then appreciate God's play.

When I pulled up at the Longhorn Motel and Restaurant, Jim came out and hugged me. He was unshaven, wild eyed, and moving fast. But he was also open and loving toward me. I hadn't been there long when our friend who managed the restaurant pulled me aside and asked, "What's wrong with Jim? We are so worried about him. Thank goodness you're here, Judy. We didn't know what to do. If the Clean Air Project is taken away from him, we're worried that he may fall apart."

Hearing this, I was even more certain that everything was falling into place. I felt confident and like the caregiver I had traveled there to be.

Jim and I drove to our casita, where he immediately cleaned up, and we made love. We had made love only once in that entire year, when I flew there in January, in the hours before he started screaming at me. This was seven months later, and Jim was both familiar and unfamiliar to me. What I felt mostly was relief at being back with him in our home.

The week proceeded well. We were very close physically, giving and receiving comfort from one another. Jim apologized over and over for all the pain he had caused me. "I am in love with you again, Judy Eron. I can see how safe you are. Why I had to turn on you, I don't understand. And on the matter of other women—that was just my attempt to dilute your effect on me. You are always so deep in me."

Yet silently, I was assessing Jim's condition. He was moving fast, interrupting, and intruding into other people's conversations. He had trouble listening and was still inflating his accomplishments; I was embarrassed for him. Jim's attitude was one of "I know it all, and so much better than you do." He kept repeating that everyone thought he was fine, which was absurd given that several people had approached me with great concern for Jim's mental state. But I didn't tell him that. I was on thin ice and determined to keep skating. I suppose that I was wanting to love Jim back into being healthy enough to choose to take lithium again.

Early in the visit, Jim expressed a wish to leave the ranch for a while and travel with me in my upcoming move to New York, then maybe elsewhere. I had spent an entire year wanting nothing else but for Jim to want to be with me. Yet now it was unsettling for me that he wanted to accompany me to New York, as I knew that I'd be dealing with my own anxiety about the move. Jim had always been very reactive to my anxiety even when he was healthy. I could only imagine what he would be like in his present condition with the myriad decisions that I'd be facing.

However, I let it be and just said, "Well, Jim, let's see." But he went ahead as though plans were already made. I would hear him on the phone with his brother or various others saying, "I'll be helping Judy move to New York."

Now that I was more grounded and back on Jim's team, I could finally feel my sadness watching this wonderful man whom I so admired behaving with so little consciousness of how strangely he was acting. It hurt to see him like this.

We had several blowups, including one major one that looked like it might kill yet another visit. However, this time Jim eventually took responsibility for his part in the explosion. He told me, "I feel ashamed and humbled, Judy. You hang in with me so fiercely. You try so hard."

The blowups were over money, who should pay for the repairs and insurance on the house given that it still belonged to both of us (though Jim would receive it in the divorce in just a few weeks) and what had been decided about the value of Bernice, our defunct truck. This one got especially heated, with Jim accusatory, even ferocious when I tried to stand my ground.

When this happened on one of our walks, I turned and went back to the house, with Jim yelling after me. Once at the house, I made a decision to just "eat it," to apologize and split the difference of our dispute about value. When Jim arrived back at the house, I told him, "Jim, I'm sorry. I want us to get along. Let's just—"

"Judith, this is not forgivable. You might as well just pack and leave. We cannot resolve this. You are clearly too hung up on pinching every penny out of me that you can, and I cannot live with that. You disgust me."

"Jim, please don't do this."

"Judith, stay away from me."

Then he went back in the house and came out with a notebook of his poems. "Do you want to know how I feel? I wrote this last October, Judith. Last October. You're so sure you know how I feel—well, read this."

And I read it. I wept as I read his poem about how little his experiences and successes meant if I was not part of them.

"I didn't know, Jim. It makes me so sad, so sorry."

Somehow that softened him again. "Thank you, Judy. Yes, it makes me sad, too."

This exchange got us back to a good place. Again and again on this visit, Jim expressed his gratitude to me for leading us to softness and union. That had always been one of the things I treasured most about Jim, that he noticed and appreciated whatever efforts I made.

Although I remained hesitant, I finally did agree for Jim to come to Nashville to help me with my move to New York. He was so grateful for my coming to the casita to help him, he wanted to return the kindness. As he was gaining clarity, he was thanking me for still loving him, and he was taking responsibility for some of what had happened during the year. I now recognize that Jim was beginning to spiral downward, which allowed him to have more awareness of what he had been doing and the damage he had caused, the people he had alienated. I wasn't aware of it then because Jim still appeared so manic, but his brain chemistry must have been moving toward depression.

I left Texas on August 20 and had a week before Jim arrived in Nashville. We spoke several times, and he left many messages giving me his whereabouts. Our talks were brief and rather matter-of-fact, lacking the "can you believe that we're really planning together again!" aspect that I wished for. I refrained from most sweet talk, trying to keep the amount of distance that I thought would help Jim feel safe. In fact, every step I took in the interval between our reunion and his death was measured, with me always trying to modulate the intensity of my interactions with him.

I am not sure this came from any wisdom or was any help.

I had pledged myself to begin school even if Jim and I were to be fully reunited. I wanted nothing more than to return with him to the desert to resume our former life. But I knew he needed to be back on medication, and even love struck and starry-eyed, I could see that Jim was not to be counted on as I had done before. At the very least, we had to go slowly with one another. It seemed almost a blessing that nothing really had to be decided since he was needing to be in Texas for several photography workshops and I was needing to be in New York City for school.

Jim's trip to Nashville took him through Alpine on August 28 where he actually had to appear in court for our divorce. It was such a grand irony that on his way to bring us together, Jim had to stop off to pull us apart. (By some fluke, the divorce was not recorded in the courthouse until September 10, which became significant after Jim's death.)

I picked Jim up at the airport, and we smiled and hugged. Not our former burst of affection, but just fine when compared to our meetings of the past year when Jim was furious and barely let me touch him.

When we got to the work of packing my belongings, there were many decisions to make, such as what size U-Haul to rent and how to secure my motorcycle. Jim stayed calm and helpful, as he had promised. Even when I contradicted his opinion on how to fasten things, he went along with my position. I had been quite explicit with him about my concern that my anxiety would disgruntle him, and Jim had promised firmly that he would just be there for me.

Jim often repeated his stated mission, to return the favor of my coming to help him in Texas. What I'm fairly sure of now is that what he mostly wanted was just to be with me, to feel safe and loved in a context that was familiar to him. I think that he was needing to get out of the life he was living in Texas and to return to a life with me, wherever that was to be.

Realizing that now and knowing where his sadness and lost feelings led him, I am grateful that I said yes to his coming to help me, grateful that Jim had the chance to once again feel useful and kind to me, that he was able to be there for me, just as he said he would. And of course, I'm grateful I could experience that Jim again.

Jim and I had many friends in Nashville, and yet we saw only one person together, my musician friend, Pablo, and that was only for me to return something. We avoided everyone else.

We slept at Sadie's house in the lonely bed I had slept in all that year and loved each other through the night. The next morning, we left for New York. Jim drove the U-Haul, and I drove the Jeep, which gave us needed time out from each other.

Our trip included two nights in motels, eating take-out food in front of the TV as we had always loved to do. We had some car trouble and had to get a new alternator for the Jeep, but even that went smoothly. Jim was keeping his word to be supportive of me.

That Saturday night, August 30, we were staying at a motel when we heard the news of Princess Diana's crash and the next morning we read of her death. This news was jolting and unsettling. Once we hit New York, Jim became very taken with the murals that had been painted in a matter of hours and the portraits and flowers that were placed under these as altars. It now sits strangely with me that he became so preoccupied with her death just six weeks before his own.

Jim and I arrived in New York on Sunday morning,

August 31, after dropping the Jeep at my aunt and uncle's house in New Jersey. Three of my New York City cousins met us at my new apartment. Jim had been quite close with all of them, and this was the first time he had seen any of them since The Bad Year had begun. He had been terribly hurt and angry when they had written letters to him the previous autumn urging him to get back on his medicine. In his phoning frenzy of that past week, he had called each of them and reconnected; but he was still upset with them.

With his excellent eye for design, Jim arranged my tiny apartment. It came together quite quickly so we ended up having day after day to have fun exploring the city. I had bits and pieces of school that week, but no work to do. After a year of feeling I had nothing, I suddenly could anticipate having the best of everything—school and Jim.

Yet I was aware of not wanting Jim to meet my new school friends or teachers. I was realistic enough to know that I couldn't trust him to be appropriate—not talk too much or be too uncensored or too familiar with people. We did have dinner with my cousin, Frances, and she and Jim were sweet to each other. In fact, to my surprise, Jim brought Frances a gift of some little metal figurines. He told Frances to select one and give it to him to keep. She wondered whether he meant for her to choose the one she liked best or the one she liked least. In the end, she chose the one she liked best, an eagle. I found this eagle on Jim's desk in Texas after he died and am looking at it on my desk now as I write this.

We had some great times that week. We took the subway to Yankee Stadium for a baseball game and to

Coney Island where we sat on the beach in the blowing September sand. We picked up the Jeep in New Jersey and drove to watch a football game with Jim's son. Jim found a place for us to play pool near my apartment, and he selected restaurants—it was really a wonderful time. Jim seemed happy.

We had lots of warm and close affection and sex. Soft music and sweet sex and the wonderful view of New York from my windows.

We also had a few difficult talks. Jim was uncensored, speaking about how nonmonogamy was more natural, but monogamy more practical. He spoke about lithium and about the summer of '96. I did my best to not comment on either. He wanted me to be open with him about any sexual encounters I'd had. Since there was very little to tell, I gave only sparse details. Any of these topics could have ignited into a huge conflagration, but somehow we kept them contained.

Over and over, when I thought about Jim's returning to Texas, it seemed like a good thing to me. It was clear that he was not the old Jim, that he needed to be on medicine and was still walking the edge. I kept all this to myself, which felt like lying to him and concerned me greatly. How could we possibly rebuild our relationship if we weren't—if I wasn't—honest? I had no solution other than to keep hoping that Jim would crash and be receptive to taking medicine again. I knew I wanted to be back with him and for us to be married again eventually. It had been so awful for me all year to be separated from him. But for now, I was glad that we would be living apart, especially if we could keep this closeness and affection.

Obviously I was not willing to take the risk of being forthright with Jim about medication. I was not open with him about my certainty that he was manic-depressive and needed to be back on a mood stabilizer. I simply did not want to risk losing him again.

The day before Jim was to leave, as we lay in bed, he told me, "Judy, I feel scared. I'm anxious about leaving you. I'm anxious about what my life is and what I'll do with myself. I need to do a big project, organizing my photographs. I'm going to a workshop on infrared photography soon in Santa Fe. But I'm scared to leave you. I feel safe with you."

I did not know what to say. I wanted us to be together, but I was churning with the dishonesty of not telling him that I felt he should be back on lithium. For me, it felt right for him to go back to Texas for the time being. I assumed we would make plans for him to come back to New York soon.

He was supposed to leave on Friday, but I urged him to stay through the weekend, which he did. He made several calls to people on the ranch to reassure himself that they were still in his life. Minna apparently was pleasant on the phone (but then rejected him again as soon as she saw him the next day).

On Monday morning, September 8, we arose early, and I accompanied Jim on the bus to LaGuardia Airport. There, we had a swift, tearful parting.

"I love you, Jim."

"I love you, Judy."

That was the last time I ever saw him.

...MUST COME DOWN

Part Two: September 8, 1997 – October 11, 1997

You're Soaring

You tried to fly too fast, and you tried to fly too high.
But you forgot to take your engines when you went up in the sky;
And so you landed, not gently,
On the ground, the very hard ground.

You thought you'd just get up. You thought you'd just brush off.
You thought you'd prove to everyone that you could stay aloft,
And we were watching, but we couldn't catch you,
As you crashed down.

Chorus:
But now you're flying, you're soaring. I hear your engines
roaring,
As you navigate your way to heaven's door.
You're sweeping, you're swooping, you're even loop-de-looping,
With no need for any caution anymore.

So, Baby, just have fun up there—for that you have a knack.
Wave as you fly over, and I promise I'll wave back.
And just be reckless, be triumphant,
And be free.

Chorus:
'Cause now you're flying, you're soaring. I hear your engines
roaring,
As you navigate your way to heaven's door.
You're sweeping, you're swooping, you're even loop-de-looping,
With no need for any caution anymore.

You tried to fly too fast, and you tried to fly too high.
But you forgot to take your engines when you went up in the sky.
But now be reckless, be triumphant,
And be free.
And know I love you, as I know you're loving me.

Song by Judy Eron
Written October 14, 1997

13

THE BEGINNING OF THE END

Looking back, I see now that Jim's brain chemistry had already begun to change when he called me to come be with him in Texas. That's why he was able to call me and to think differently about me. Certainly, much of his behavior was still manic—pressured speech, tangential thinking, flight of ideas, numerous phone calls. But something was changing that was allowing him space for thoughts and insights that he had been unable to have during the previous year—painful thoughts, painful insights. He was beginning to see the possibility that he was responsible for his relationship messes, and that brought on shame and, for the first time in a year, guilt.

Once Jim returned to the casita from New York City, his mood and behavior seemed to change, quickly and abruptly. I couldn't count on his feelings holding from one call to the next. At first, he was more aloof, back to business. Then he called frequently, leaving many messages about us, just checking in, trying to stay connected. He sounded looser on the phone, his thoughts darting from topic to topic. He was more grandiose, and I wasn't thinking depression at all, but rather that Jim was getting higher and more manic again.

I questioned myself continually about how Jim and I could be partnered if he remained off his medicine. I reassured myself that nothing needed to be decided, that things were safe and solid with me living in New York and Jim in Texas. It could be quite nice, actually, having the excitement of both places in our joint lives, with each of us having a reason to be in a separate place from the other for the time being.

In my heart and my more rational self, I knew that for us to have a future together, a life we could count on, Jim's illness would have to be under control, which meant medication. Eventually we would have to agree that he had manic-depressive illness and that medication was the only way for us to live with it, for there to be an "us."

But for now, with two thousand miles separating us, I felt safe trying to be close emotionally. Although Jim was still off medication, I felt better now that he no longer considered me his enemy.

When we came back together in Texas, Jim and I had agreed not to talk to his family about us. He had felt betrayed by my staying close with his brother and sister and parents. It was important to me to demonstrate to him that now it was just the two of us working things out.

In retrospect, that was a bad idea. Jim was still sick, and I was still vulnerable and not a strong decision maker. He would not have agreed, but we needed his family's help. I see now that this was another time I let my need for connection with Jim override my better judgment. All the confusion I had experienced during The Bad Year had shaken me and left me vulnerable to that need.

School was both interesting and demanding, but I missed Jim and stayed preoccupied with him. We spoke frequently, and it took a lot of energy to filter what I said to him and to contain my need to gush over him as I used to do. I was having to gear down my expectations. I wanted to tell Jim about my new experiences, but he did not have the ability to focus on me.

As I had been doing all year, I took notes as thoroughly as I could when we spoke on the phone. Reviewing our conversations later sometimes helped me feel less confused, and I could refer back to these notes, to try to understand what was going on.

Excerpts from this period of my journal follow, full of the push and pull from Jim and my own jumble of responses.

Wednesday, September 10, 1997
Three phone calls from Jim. He leaves tomorrow for his photography workshop in Santa Fe. He says our divorce got filed today, but we can get undivorced if we want to, within thirty days of today. "I just wanted to mention it," he said.

Jim suggests we create a fund of money jointly to

pay for phone calls. This would be much like ten years ago when he led us to create an account for our recreation as a way to begin handling money together.

My reaction: "But, Jim, you've been so critical of me about money all year."

Jim: "Judy, can't you see that that was all my projections? I have always respected you about money and property. You are wise and generous. Forget what I said."

And he wants us to do a project together, probably photography and music. I love Jim not being hostile. But he does not seem whole to me.

Monday, September 15

A package of papers from Jim. He says he wants me to know him. And yet it looks so hodgepodge, his inner working.

Wednesday, September 17, 9:30 A.M.
(Phone call from Jim)

Jim: Judy, this is my stuff. This is not you. Can you do that? Can you listen to this?

Judy: I'll try.

Jim: My paranoia is quite high. The water pump is broken, the electrical is down. It is stressful on me. I've got a lot of stress. The Washington State taxes aren't paid, I let them slip. And the mutual funds process that my investment guy did didn't work.

Judy: Just put it all in an envelope, and I'll take care of it. I can share the load with you, Jim. You aren't alone.

Jim: My fear of caving into depression is real now. This is more difficult to talk about, my feelings for you, what I've done. And now that we're doing well, I ask myself, "What the fuck have you done, Jim?"

(I cry.)

Jim: Judy, I'm looking at me as a manic person. Now with this confusion and the air-pollution thing.

Judy: I don't know how to respond to you, Jim.

Jim: This is a different time, Judy. It won't be as lyrical. Judy, we listen to Jim, right? And only you and I are talking, right? There are no others, right?

Judy: Yes, Jim. Jim, "Big D-Depression," what if you feel that? I want you to tell me so we can get you up here, Jim. *(I want to mention medication, but I don't.)*

Jim: This Diane character at the Santa Fe workshop, she is very attractive. But I'm interested in you, Judy. Another time, I would've been interested in her. But you and I have made a peace, so some of my energy is toward you, Judy. My anger that was fueling me is gone, and I am less. I had met Diane before, and I was attracted to her before. I'm trying to say something comforting to you, Judy. I think I want you, Judy . . . I don't have my anger, so then I say to myself, "Where have you been, Jim? Everybody's been telling you, Jim, that Judy is good, and that's not the problem. Judy is okay." So I must be crazy. And this is how I'm inclined to look at this past year. So it makes me sad, and it makes me scared. As we make peace, I ask, "Why, why, why then, Jim, this circuitous, high-energy, low-efficiency time?" And I say to myself, "Jim, this is craziness that I know you have." Judy, I wish I could express to you the hurt in my heart for things that I caused you. You bring that from you, Judy. With your heart.

Judy: *(I weep.)* I want to be with you, Jim. I want to hold you and have you not be there alone. I want you to not have to dissolve as you feel peace with me.

Saturday, September 20, 10:30 P.M.
(Phone call from Jim)

Jim: I'm in a different mental state, Judy. I'm anxious, not depressed. The air-pollution work is over. There is much turmoil between people, and I suffer from that. It looks to others like my work was self-aggrandizing. I feel unappreciated and abused. And the whole thing with Minna . . . I am feeling a lethargy. Not restful. I've experienced this before, the anxiety before depression. It gets me into familial thinking. For example, are we like my parents, that when one is up, the other is down? My year was not enjoyable, but at least it was enthusiastic. And you were down. And now I am down, and you are more up.

Judy: Jim, do you feel like traveling, coming up here?

Jim: No, I feel inclined to become a hermit in a passive, lethargic way. Basically, Judy, I need to set-

tle more with you. I want to come toward you.
There is so much self-castigation I can do for my
treatment of you. You are of the utmost value to
me and have always been. My negativity
obscured it all year, and now it isn't. I want you
to do what you are doing, Judy. As bad as you've
been with heartache, you've not lain down.
You're a model. Moving has been good for me in
the past, so I want to come to New York.

Judy: Jim, get in the car right now, and come here.

Jim: I'll wait and see how I feel tomorrow. I will not
interfere with what you are doing. The level of
injustice would be heinous. My purpose in coming to New York would be first to create movement. And second, I need some counsel. Quite
frankly, there is no one except you. I need to figure what to do now. When we stand back, Judy,
and look at this, this is another real important
time in my life. I don't want to repeat old pat-
terns. I want to rejoin you and to continue to
rejoin.

Judy: How scared are you that I wouldn't be here for
you, Jim?

Jim: Enough. I say to myself, "What is with you, Jim?
Why would you feel this and do this now, Jim?"
Am I fucking with you, Judy? Trying to sabotage
you? Three months ago, this would've been easier.
I'm in a need state. I have a bad cold. If I hadn't
gotten physically sick, maybe this wouldn't be
happening. I need to see you for counsel. I just
need to see you, Judy. I need help figuring about

173

us, figuring about me. The decision I need to make: Either this last year has been gross pathology and I should be on lithium, or what has been happening has been chaotic, but growthful. And whoever has come in contact with me has had a price to pay. To go under psychiatric care requires a retrenching I don't want to do. How do I desire to live and conceive of my life?

Hearing all his self-questioning was music to my ears, in a way. But it was also incredibly sad; Jim is so lost and needy. I feel too far away from him. I want to be able to hold him and soothe him, to receive his apologies, to say whatever he needs to hear about my forgiving him, and to help him feel he has a future to move into, a future with me that would be safe, even with this illness.

Monday, September 22

Spoke with Jim. He is not inclined to come now, after all. He wants to try to "dig in" there.

It hit me. I felt the effect of my being in the dance with him. I am sensitive to his pulling back again. And I can see the importance of my not getting on any playing field with him where anything—ANYTHING—will depend on him.

I am sick of this. I want him back, *really* back.

Thursday, September 25

My uncle, Leon, died. We had the funeral. But I was unable to reach Jim, he hadn't answered my calls for two days. He finally called back, and it turns out that the old VW he bought broke down again, and he was stuck in Alpine, had to get a ride back to the ranch. His vehicle situation is pathetic.

He says he misses me and loves me. But he is depressed. More silent.

Frances is going away for two weeks in October. I invited Jim to come to New York, we could stay in her apartment. Perhaps I can find him something (what?) to do. I contacted the Fashion Institute of Technology, and they are sending me a list of photography classes he might take.

I worried and worried when I couldn't reach him. He is not doing well.

Saturday, September 27

I am so sad and lonely and feel so unsafe sharing my sadness and loneliness with Jim. I called him to say hello earlier today. Left a message. He left a message back, and I just called him. He says he's okay. But it is a nothing call. Flat.

"I don't know if I can be what you need me to be right now, Judy."

Wednesday, October 1

I miss Jim so desperately, and we haven't spoken since Saturday, and I am disturbed. He could be:
a) fine and busy
b) depressed and in bed
c) stuck somewhere with no vehicle
d) on his way here
e) in the hospital
f) trying medicine, privately
g) with a woman

I am sad. I am scared. I am angry. I am lonely. Can there be a "happy ending" here, a segue into a more normal connection between us?

I am "chasing" him, trying to stay connected to my husband who is mentally ill.

Midnight. I left another message for him. Where is he? I pray he is on his way here or on his way to medication. I ache for him.

Thursday, October 2

Still no word from Jim. Since Saturday. I am preoccupied and worried. I also keep hoping and wanting to see Jim show up here, to know I am here for him.

Where is he?

Friday, October 3

8:45 P.M. I finally called Jim's friends, Toby and Shayne, the only two left on the ranch that I know Jim was still trusting at last report. They drove the two-hour round trip and said the house was wide open and Jim wasn't around, as though he had left quickly. Was he hiding when they came? They left him a note to call me or them.

Jim left me this message on my machine just now: "I just got back, and Toby and Shayne left me a note, something about you being worried." He sounded pissed off.

Now I'm a nervous wreck. Not good. I'm back to my own fear and anxiety from this whole last year before Jim turned to me again. I am so afraid of alienating him.

11 P.M. I've been going back and forth, why it's okay to call Jim versus why it's an intrusion, and I finally called him. Miraculously, he answered the phone. Pretty mute. However, mercifully, he said he understands my dilemma about calling him, sending someone to check on him.

"Jim, do you want me to come be with you? Please let me come."

"No."

"Do you want to come here?"

"No."

I was weeping, feeling utterly helpless. I told him that I'm loving him, I'm here, that he can't get rid of me. I asked whether he is getting out to get his mail, and he said no. So he is missing all I am sending him—daily letters, and tapes of my songs and classwork, trying to keep him knowing how involved I am with him.

"Are you listening to phone messages, Jim, on your machine?"

"Sometimes."

"Are you eating?"

He answered with irritation. "Of course. Don't ask me questions."

I kept crying. "But Jim, I felt invited back into your life, and now I'm flat out. I don't know what to do."

"I don't know how to advise you," he said without feeling. "This is a time I'm uncommunicative. I'll just have to get through this time."

"Would you please just leave me a message every day or so that you're okay? Just say your name, that's all, into my machine."

"I don't know if I can keep that obligation, Judy."

I cried and cried, not knowing what to say to him. And then I said, "I love you, Jim." Silence. "Good-bye, Jim."

"Good-bye."

Sunday, October 5, 1 A.M.

I married my beloved Jim ten years ago today. I remember wrestling with the rightness of marrying him the night before we married, a little cold feet. I never knew what I was in for, marrying him.

I cannot reach him. His phone was busy for hours today, and I'm sure that he had it off the hook on purpose, not wanting to talk. Now his answering machine is off, so the phone rings and rings and rings. And rings.

I had a horrible morning and early evening. I finally spoke with Roy, breaking the agreement not to talk with Jim's family. Roy pressured me to go to Texas and scope out Jim's situation. I want his mother or his brothers to go with me. I don't want to make Jim hate me again, as he has all year. I feel I am walking such a delicate balance.

This is so hard. What is the "responsible" thing to do? What is best for Jim? Does he have internal wisdom? Or is he metaphorically hanging out in the Greyhound bus station?

12 noon. I'm at the State Line Lookout on the Palisades Parkway in New Jersey. Rode my motorcycle. A surprise that the fall colors are happening. I'm in my Terlingua Ranch sweatshirt, a gift from Jim, and the dolphin crystal necklace he gave me, on a silk cord that I always wear.

One friend suggested I should take my helplessness and nervous energy and line up emergency mental health assistance in Alpine. I said no. If and when he gets depleted, psychotic, then I'll go with his brother and get him. I just couldn't and wouldn't call the police to go get him. It would be too much of a violation.

178

Someone else would have to do that.

My plan: Give Jim until Wednesday to contact me—three days. Then I will feel free to call his other brothers and whomever feels important on *my* team. *My* team is *our* team, even if he doesn't believe that.

Then on Thursday I will call Toby and Shayne and ask them to go check on Jim again. I will offer to pay for gas or whatever. And I will tell them about his depression.

I will not go down there now. And I will hope he calls with just "It's Jim" on the message machine. Or with "Please come, Judy."

There have been many miracles in the past two months. So who am I to question where this is going?

Midnight

Dearest Jim,

It's just now turning from October 5 to October 6, and I am keenly aware of it being ten years since we got married. I loved you then, Jim, and I love you now. I want you in my arms this moment, to hold you and smell you. I am worried being so distant from you, but I am trying to respect your process.

Truly, I don't know what to do but hold you in my heart and try to keep connected.

Monday, October 6

This is what we've waited for, for more than a year. It seems we have to let Jim get very low and ready for compliance.

10 P.M. Jim's mother called me tonight. She herself is obviously still quite depressed. She was calling to say that she couldn't reach Jim despite calling him at many different times. So I spilled the beans several days earlier than I was going to, told her he is depressed and out of touch. She feels it is imperative that Jim get on medication and that people in Texas know what is happening.

She said, "It's an empty place he's in, Judy."

I said, "You know a lot about that."

"Yes, I do, Judy. I'm still in it."

"Do you think you could help Jim?"

"Possibly so."

I told her that I walk a line of not wanting to ruin a future for me and Jim, which I'm afraid intruding on him would do.

Anyway, that's tonight's report. I called Roy, and he pushed me that he wants to tell his brothers if they call. I said, "Refer them to me if they call, and I'll make this silence all my fault. I just want to not put everybody on alarm. I am trying to respect Jim's privacy."

Wednesday, October 8, midnight

Very worried. Am I ignoring the obvious, that Jim says I'm his most important person, so maybe he is worried that I won't forgive him? If so, that is his call for me to come to him.

Or is it the very opposite? Cass called me. I told her what is happening.

I called Toby and Shayne to ask if they would go check on Jim again, and I finally told them a little about Jim's depression. I said I'm trying to protect Jim's privacy, but that I think he needs medicine. Shayne says she'll go tomorrow morning and check. I asked her to check the refrigerator to see if he has food. I also told her I don't expect her to do anything but check on him.

I finally called Jim's other brothers and told them

about these past weeks. No decisions.

Thursday, October 9, 6 A.M.

I awake with a dream that I call and Jim answers the phone.

It's also possible that Jim is okay, living some life. My only wish is to know he's alive.

(Note: It is upsetting now to read these words since I do not have memory of actually being afraid that Jim would kill himself. Quite the opposite. When I mentioned to one of Jim's brothers that he had a shotgun in the house, I felt I was being hysterical, unnecessarily dramatic. I weep now for my poor, well-intentioned self. Ultimately, unintentionally, my respect for and fear of Jim helped to facilitate his isolation and death.)

11 A.M. Between classes, I called Toby and Shayne. They didn't go and can't go until Monday.

I was so anxious when I called. Every minute since Sunday when Jim shut off his answering machine has been directed toward the relief of another report on him. It was such a letdown that they didn't drive up to check on him.

Late for class, but thinking I should fly down to Texas right away. Then I called Carl, another person we know on the ranch, to ask if he would please go check on Jim. But all I got was his answering machine. I left a message.

I went to class, shaking, teary, distracted. I told one of my classmates who knows a little about my situation with Jim, and he said, "I really don't think you should go. I'm afraid that you'll end up staying there and not come back to school. You're much too talented to let this program go." I don't think that I will give up school if I go, but I feel a compelling pull, an intense need to DO something, and all I can actually DO is go to Jim.

I spoke with Cass again. I felt unsure whether to call Jim's sons to tell them that their dad is depressed and isolating himself. Cass urged me to wait, that for them to know about his depression could be so interruptive of Jim's newly healed relationship with them and his desire for their respect.

Friday, October 10, 9:45 A.M.

I called Carl several more times, no answer. I need to call someone to check on Jim, but I don't know who would feel least like a violation to him besides Toby and Shayne.

Plan: Wait and see if Toby and Shayne can go on Monday. If not, then call the ranch manager and advise him that Jim is depressed since our divorce and I can't reach him. I don't have to mention manic-depression. (*Note: Here I am, still protecting Jim's privacy, the very evening before his suicide.*)

Midnight. Carl left a message on my machine that he sent someone to check on Jim and he wasn't there, but the cats are being tended. The message was confusing, like Jim was gone and having someone feed the cats. Does that mean his truck wasn't there? Could he be headed here?

I keep looking out my window hoping to see Jim in the park, hoping to see his truck.

When he was a street person in 1982, he ate, shaved, stayed dry, slept. He took care of himself then. He is probably doing that now.

Dearest Jim,

I love you. I wish you knew how deliberate I have tried to be all year to protect your privacy and dignity. But it's impossible to not fail at.

It is Yom Kippur now, as today becomes tomorrow. Day of Atonement. I beg your forgiveness for my transgressions.

Saturday, October 11, 8:45 A.M. YOM KIPPUR

I write this looking out over the cliffs of the Hudson River. It's chilly, and I rode my motorcycle up here. It's too early, and I'm underdressed and cold, and the coffee shop is not open. It's autumn. A crisp clear day.

I called the ranch office to see if they knew anything more from the person who went to check on Jim yesterday. They said that Toby and Minna are going up to check on Jim this morning.

Last Yom Kippur was in Hawaii. So much pain. I was so hoping to be able to erase those pains, those memories. But I now have new sadnesses, new worries.

Mary wondered aloud yesterday about my future with Jim—that this may be life with him. Which I cannot endure. A life with never knowing if he'll be present, physically or emotionally.

Just a few weeks ago, I was his long true love. We were talking about how we could benefit from and enjoy his being in Texas, my being in New York. He wanted a fund for phone calls. It was about connection. But the connection dissolved so quickly and so thoroughly. So now what?

As for the Day of Atonement, it's true that I take it seriously, wanting to have this day be special and important. To feel a new beginning to this next year. To restart with Jim.

I've been mailing Jim a letter or card every day, and today I already mailed one, but I'll write another and mail it.

Hi Jim,

I'm on the Palisades Parkway. I miss you. I called you from a pay phone here. It rang and rang and I spoke to the ringing as though it were you. I was not dry-eyed.

I had you back, your love and connection if not fully you, just three weeks ago. And now you are fully dissolved again.

2 P.M. Jim is dead.

14

THE END OF THE BEGINNING

Jim died on October 11, 1997, sometime in the early hours of the morning.

I returned from my motorcycle ride around 11 A.M., dropping off that last note to Jim in the mailbox across the street from my apartment. I called the ranch, and they said that Toby and Minna had not yet gone up to the house.

I took a hot bath. As I took off my clothes, I found that the crystal dolphin necklace that Jim had sent me the month before, and which I always wore, had come untied and was loose inside my shirt. Its silk cord had never come undone before and has never since. Not to be too airy-fairy, but I believe that this was Jim's good-bye to me.

The phone call came around 2 P.M. I was sitting at my desk trying to concentrate on writing a scene and a song for school. The scene was about a man with an incurable illness contemplating suicide.

I picked up the phone and heard the voice of a neighbor of ours at the ranch. The phone call was absolutely unexpected, and yet I felt like I was in a movie with an inevitable plot line.

How do you tell someone her husband has killed himself? She began with "Judy, you need to sit down. I have something bad to tell you." She then kept repeating these preparatory statements. "Something bad has happened that I need to tell you. Judy, you need to sit down. I am going to tell you something bad."

As her preface was rambling on, I was getting it. She hadn't said it yet, but I was understanding that Jim was dead. Nonetheless, inside every second of comprehension of this knowledge that he was dead was a hope, a desperate wish that she would say, "Jim is in the hospital, critical, but alive. You need to come quickly."

Or better yet, my longed-for wish: "Jim is running around naked in the road, clucking like a chicken."

But that's not what she said. Actually I don't remember exactly what she said, but probably it was, "Jim has shot himself. He is dead, Judy." I seem to remember a split second when it was possible that he wasn't dead. Between the "himself" at the end of the first sentence, and the "He" that began the next sentence, there was a possibility, however small, that he wasn't dead.

But he was dead. Unbelievably, irreversibly dead.

I hung up and immediately called my cousin, Frances. She lived about a mile away from my apartment, and she headed over right away.

While I waited for Frances, I called Roy, who was not

home, and Cass, who was. Cass's "Oh, no!" said it all. I then called Jim's two other brothers, only reaching one. I think I was quick about it, got right off the phone. "I have to go." I was extremely agitated, paced, punched the wall, screamed. I was living in a small apartment, next to, across from, above, and below other people, and I was screaming. But New York is New York, and probably no one noticed.

I tried to reach Jim's sons. Neither one answered the phone, so I had to leave a message, just telling them to call Cass as soon as they got this message. It was very strange leaving messages, knowing that people would be getting news soon that would alter their lives forever.

Frances arrived, and I yelled at her. "We were wrong, Frances. We were wrong. We thought he would not kill himself, and we were wrong. Waiting for him to get 'depressed enough'—what were we thinking? We were wrong, and now he's dead."

Frances is a very sensitive person so I kept apologizing, but I kept yelling at her. I wasn't crying at all, just yelling and pacing.

Then my brother called from Hawaii. Frances had called our cousin, Alan, who also lived in New York City, and Alan had called my brother.

"I'm so sorry, Judy."

"Larry, what should I do?"

"You should go to Texas, Judy."

"Why?"

"Out of respect." (I don't really understand the sense of this remark now, but at the time it made perfect sense.)

"Will you go with me, Larry?"

"I wish I could, but I can't. What about Jim's brother and sister?"

"Yes, that's it. I'll ask them to go. I'll go there, I'll go to Ohio."

It instantly became clear what I would do. Of course I wanted to be with Jim's family in Ohio—his brother, sister, and parents. I called the airlines and began the process to fly to Ohio immediately.

I realized I would need to garage my motorcycle, which was parked on the street and required moving twice a week due to street-cleaning ordinances. So in the midst of my tears and anguish, I rode my motorcycle over to a parking garage I knew.

I ran back to my apartment, maybe a half mile, carrying my helmet, wailing, but still not crying. Thankfully, my shock and grief were invisible in New York. Frances met me at the door to say that Alan and his wife, Hiroko, had come. Alan hugged me, but it was Hiroko's embrace that finally helped me to cry. Why Hiroko, I can't say. But I wept in her small arms.

My three cousins helped pack me, with me yelling at Frances that she was doing it wrong. The abuse she took from me is embarrassing to remember now. But I was in shock, and I was screaming for control of something, anything. A reason to blame someone for something. So I blamed Frances for the way she was packing my clothes.

Frances, Alan, and Hiroko took me in a taxi to LaGuardia Airport. My cousins. They had all loved Jim, and they had all been targets of his fury and venom during The Bad Year. Then they had all stretched to forgive him when he helped me move to New York. Alan's being with me was especially poignant because Alan's father, my uncle, had killed himself thirty-five years before.

Then suddenly I was alone on the plane with only my tears for company. It is strange but true that I spent my flight rewriting a scene and song, my assignment for school I had been in the middle of doing when The Call had come. Somehow, on the plane, it was precisely what I could concentrate on that would keep me away from the reality of what my life had now become.

It was late night when Roy and Cass met me at Dayton Airport. We three held each other there at the gate, Cass and I weeping fiercely. A long cry. The drive to Cass's house where I always stayed was filled with tears and question marks—disbelief, grief, and more grief.

At my brother's suggestion, I took some Benadryl so that I would be too fatigued to not sleep. It worked, although I awoke very early. I ran over to Roy's house, where he held me as I wept and wept and wept.

Once the sun was up, it was time for me to go to Jim's parents who lived next door to Roy. They were still in bed together, and when she saw me, his mother started to cry. We held each other, weeping, heaving. Then his father wept, and they held each other. It was an intensely sad and tender moment with them, this eighty-one-year-old couple who had just lost a child.

Roy and I planned our trip to Texas for the next day. I felt an urgency to be there. Roy was deciding whether he wanted to see Jim's body, which would have meant a stop in San Antonio where the autopsy was being performed. Jim's sons and I finally spoke, and I urged them to come to Ohio, but they had decided to meet us in Texas. There was much planning and many, many phone calls.

One of the many difficult things for me during those first days—hell, even now—is that Jim and I were divorced. The thirty days in which we could have undone the divorce had expired two days before Jim died. Technically, I was not even his widow. Hence, the decisions about how to deal with his death were not mine to make, legally, even though I knew everything about what Jim had wanted. We had talked about this in depth.

I'll digress here for a moment to tell why we had talked so seriously about death and in such detail even though we were only in our forties, healthy, and had no young children. When we had known each other for just three months, we took a trip out West, Jim's very first trip to the desert. The time we had was exquisitely intense, and on one particular walk, we mentioned death for some reason. Jim burst out crying, weeping with big, deep sobs.

"Jim, what's wrong?" I asked, taking him in my arms.

"Oh, Judy, if I were to lose you now that I've found you . . ." He was frightened.

I held him while he wept. This was the first time that we were each aware of what Jim called his "imprinting" on me like a baby duckling does with its mother and how tied to me he had already become. So we began what we called our "death discussions" every now and then, what would we do "if," that sort of thing. These talks were always very poignant and emotional.

Furthermore, Jim and I had both counseled people with AIDS. At that time, just about everyone with AIDS was soon to die. We talked about death with them and with each other, focusing especially on the need for preparation and for the person's wishes to be known. That's how I knew that Jim wanted to be cremated and scattered on the desert and that he did not want a service, only a gathering if it was something that I needed. I even knew what music he wanted played.

If Jim had died two days earlier, the divorce could have been undone and all the decisions would have been mine to make. And although I would have considered what Jim's sons wanted, *they* might not have had the chance to ponder what they really wanted and needed. It is important that they had this chance.

Roy and I arrived at the casita at sundown and spent time slowly looking around, shaking our heads at the order that appeared to be everywhere. This did not look like the home of someone depressed. The house was as neat as Jim had always kept things, not exactly spic and span, but neat, and work was spread out on his big table along with his leather folder. The phones were plugged in, ringers on, although the answering machine was off. I had expected the phones to be unplugged since I had been calling Jim many times each day and had never gotten an answer. It turned out that the phone must have rung and rung, and Jim must have ignored it, perhaps never really even hearing it through his depression.

The only "clues" or possible evidence of Jim's preplanning that we found were these: 1) Martha the cat and her three untamed kittens were outside, and there was a large pan of food for them. Usually they lived indoors and ate indoors out of small bowls. 2) The battery on the truck was disconnected. Jim was not one to attend to vehicles, so it would have been unusual for him to do something like this. 3) There was no evidence of marijuana or paraphernalia anywhere although Jim owned a bong, pipes, and other gizmos. We thought perhaps he had buried them so they wouldn't be found.

Scant clues. If Jim did some preplanning, it wasn't much. He did not empty his files nor did he leave his wallet out as some people do. He was in psychic pain, he had a shotgun and shells, and he shot himself.

There was no note. The sometimes dreaded, sometimes comforting suicide note was nowhere to be found. I searched and searched even though it seemed like something he would have left out in plain view. But there was nothing.

I also kept searching his clothes, thinking that there might be something in his pockets that would help me understand what had happened. One last pocket might reveal a note or a clue.

I really don't know what I think a note could have said that would have helped. As one woman in my suicide survivors group put it, "My son left me a twelve-page letter. It didn't make him less dead."

(Even now, when I come across a file I haven't looked in for years, I wonder whether I might find something, a clue, a note.)

In her book, *Personal History*, Katherine Graham talks about her husband who also did not leave a note.

> I believe that Phil came to the sad conclusion that he would never again lead a normal life. I also

think that he realized the illness would recur . . . Phil was well aware of the damaging effects of it on others and on him. I think he felt he'd done such harm the last time around that he just couldn't deal with it, couldn't fix everything. It was unendurable to him not only that he couldn't make any of it right but that he might cause more hurt again.

I've imagined many times what Jim might have written if he had been able to express his pain or maybe what I would have wanted him to write:

Dear Judy,

I must end my life. I am so dreadfully tired of being mentally ill. I have been dealing with my unrestful mind for almost twenty years now, causing so much devastation and pain with my illness. I have scarred my sons, shamed many people over the years, hurt so many, most of all you who mean more to me than anyone ever has. I have run through your life as the fires ran through Yellowstone, laying waste to the beautiful life we made together. I have burned you, my darling, and I worry that no amount of grafting will ever make you whole again.

How can I possibly live with myself knowing this? Surely you understand that I am so deeply and darkly ashamed. I cannot even imagine asking your forgiveness.

And then there's the matter that this could very likely happen again. Judy, as you weep, please remember what this year has been like for you, what this year has done to you. Surely you would not choose to repeat that. And I could not guarantee that it would not happen again, now that it has happened at all.

Judy, my lover, my dearest, I really thought you had saved me from the horror that had been my life. I never in a million years would have guessed that my illness would make me turn away from you. But it did.

Can't you see, Judy, that I am a man not in charge of his own course? Even if I get back on medication, there still remains the chance that this could happen again. I just couldn't take it. I don't want to hurt anyone anymore. I don't want to be an infection in people's lives. I don't want to be an infection in your life.

Such a letter might have eased some of the burden of guilt I carry. It's hard to know.

Jim's sons joined Roy and me at the casita. They had stopped in San Antonio to pick up Jim's ashes. We had a memorial with our neighbors, at which I explained about Jim's manic-depressive illness. Then Jim's sons, Roy, and I made a campfire under the full moon and distributed half of Jim's ashes onto the desert. We played a tape of the two songs that Jim wanted played: "Desperado" and "Jim, You Wore a Suit Today." It felt sad and it felt holy, and I knew it was what Jim wanted.

As though in keeping with Jim's bipolar illness, the other half of Jim's ashes were buried in a military cemetery in Nashville. Although this was not part of Jim's expressed wishes, his sons wanted a grave they could visit with their children, and I understood that.

Over our years together, I wrote many songs for Jim, especially for occasions such as anniversaries and other celebrations. I felt I had to write a song for Jim on the occasion of his death. Soon after Roy and I arrived at the casita, I went off alone and wrote "You're Soaring," which I sang at all the memorials his friends and family had for him.

There was a memorial with Jim's men's group in Nashville and another with his family in Ohio. At these memorials, we played the music Jim wanted and talked about him and about our helplessness in the face of his illness. It was touching, sad, and sweet, still unbelievable to us, yet all too real.

It felt impossible to do, but I returned to New York City to continue school. Jim remained dead, along with all the hopes and possibilities our reunion had generated.

15

WOULDA, COULDA, SHOULDA

A s most people in my shoes do, I go in and out of
wondering what more I could have done than
what I did. These thoughts come in waves that
remind me of the ocean tides in Washington State where
Jim and I spent four summers. When the tide is high, it
washes up the most amazing things—dead sea lions and
sharks, sand dollars, shells, driftwood, tires, plastic bags
and bottles, and occasionally a float of some sort. Then
the water recedes, and there is an abundance of stuff left
behind that just messes up the beach. Some people like
myself pick up bits and pieces and remove them from
the beach. Most of it sits until a strong enough tide pulls
it back into the sea, to be washed back up another day;
meanwhile, it just sits and rots and smells.

So it is with my mind. The high tides bring piercing
thoughts, questions about my choices and how I han-
dled everything. Then the tide recedes, leaving the car-

casses of these questions. Some of these I examine and resolve and am able to remove from my mind. Some remain and begin to stink.

When Jim called me on October 3, responding to Shayne and Toby's note, should I have told him that I was coming and immediately gotten on a plane and flown there to be with him? Would he have killed himself that night to prevent me from seeing him depressed or from taking him to a hospital? This is the sort of question that still lies on the sand in my brain, not ready to be picked up, not washing away. It seems so necessary to answer the "should I have gone or was I wise not to go" question. I think it is important to at least consider this question, even though it is unsettling.

Such questions are, of course, natural. It seems that most if not all people who have "lost someone to suicide," as is the vernacular, carry these unanswerable questions. It is just part of the territory to feel responsible in some way, to believe that there was something else we might have done.

Other people, even many in the suicide survivors groups, interrupt any consideration of these questions with the "knee-jerk, instant potatoes" comment, "There's nothing you could have done. If a person wants to kill himself, he will find a way." To me, it's like throwing the detritus back into the sea. It's not cleaning up, really. It's just pretending it will go away. I don't like that. It's offensive to my training as a therapist and to my love for Jim. It is presumptuous to assume that Jim would still have wanted to die on Sunday if somehow he had made it through Saturday. Who can possibly know that?

I feel that it is not a bad thing for me to review the days and minutes, the thoughts and intuitions and blindness that preceded Jim's loading the shells into his shotgun, putting the barrel of that shotgun into his mouth, and pulling the trigger. I am referring to Jim's thoughts, intuitions, and blindness, as well as my own. I made choices, I called them "best guesses" about what to do or not do—*to* send people to check up on him—*not to* interrupt his solitude in wanting to try to heal himself. I need to examine these and make an assessment of them. I need to accept the ones I can and forgive myself for ones I think were well-intentioned, but poor choices. I believe this process can lead to deeper healing.

The instant potatoes people want me just to put such thoughts out of my head, tell myself that I did all I could, and move on. But how can they or anyone know whether I did everything I could have or whether I let Jim down? They don't know me, they don't know Jim, and they don't know the bond we had. What might represent "doing enough" for one of them probably would not come close to doing enough for me.

In New York City, there is a lay counselor for suicide survivors who runs a hotline. Her husband was bipolar, and she says that "in a manic fit," he responded to something she said by running past her and jumping out the window of their many-storied apartment building. This was about ten years ago, I think. She says she is "100 percent over it," that she doesn't blame herself at all.

I get her point, but something about it doesn't sit right with me. How can she be over it entirely? From my point of view, it sounds almost flaunting. I wonder if it is dangerous to her clients to hold that up as the goal, "to be over it 100 percent." That's certainly not my goal. Mine is to answer my own questions in the best way I can for myself and then to live with my conclusions. I feel I owe that to Jim—to address these questions with seriousness and compassion, and then to keep him close inside me and make it to tomorrow.

16

RECOMMENDATIONS

I'm writing this looking out at the Chisos Mountains of Big Bend National Park. It's now five years since Jim died, and I'm living in the house that he and I built together. In the divorce, Jim got the casita. When he died, his two sons inherited it. Jim's kindness and generosity shine through in these two, who returned the casita to me in 1999, two years after Jim's death.

I have remarried. Roger and I are gradually making the casita ours instead of Jim's and mine. This is not a straight path. Because Jim and I built it all, he is everywhere. Roger's courage and patience are frequently put to the test by my push-pull relationship with the past.

This book has turned out to be more of a personal narrative than I had expected. Of course I hope that you benefit from my hindsight. What follows are some conclusions and recommendations based on what I learned from my readings and my own experience.

1. Manic-depression is an illness. This is often more obvious during the depression phase when the person may clearly be unable to function. During the manic phase, it can be more difficult to stay certain that the person is ill.

2. A person who is manic may look and act strangely. But he also may be energized, sharp, and convincing, which can make it appear that he is in charge of himself and his life.

3. Mania is finite. It's easy to lose sight of this if the mania goes on and on. However, one way or another, the mania will end.

4. When the mania ends, depression almost always follows. Primarily, this involves a chemical change in the brain. But the depression may be deepened by the amount of shame the person feels once the grandiosity of the mania isn't there to prevent him from seeing the consequences of his actions.

5. Depression can be lethal. It is estimated that 15 percent of those with manic-depressive illness ultimately kill themselves.

6. You should not try to deal with mania by yourself.

7. Find a psychiatrist who knows manic-depression, and form a strong alliance with that person.

8. Join a group for people dealing with the mania of someone they love. If your spouse or partner has manic-depressive illness, find a group for couples who have dealt with the mania of one of them.

9. Some states provide for presigned hospitalization even without the clause of "danger to self or others."

It has its flaws, but should be considered if it is available to you.

10. Read, go to lectures, and study manic-depression. Become a member of the Depression and Bipolar Support Alliance (DBSA), formerly the Depression and Manic-Depression Association, and receive its mailings. Join NAMI, the National Alliance for the Mentally Ill.

11. Stay current on the latest medications and their dosages. Since Jim's death, for example, there has been some thought that a lower dosage of lithium can be effective while allowing the person to retain a little more of the energy he misses. Also, sometimes instead of taking half the daily dosage in the morning, half at night, the person can take the full dosage at night. That way, by afternoon, a person may have more energy. But you should never suggest that a person alter his medications or allow him to do so without the advice and guidance of a psychiatrist.

12. Remember that abruptly stopping lithium can trigger a manic episode.

13. I asked Kaye Jamison at a talk she gave in Princeton, New Jersey, in 2000, "What can a person do when someone she loves is manic?" She answered, "Ask the woman next to you—she's my mother." Indeed, her mother was sitting right next to me. Dr. Jamison then added, "When your loved one is already manic, there's nothing you can do except take care of yourself." (At the same time, Dr. Jamison is not suggesting that you not seek help from friends, family, or the medical community.)

14. There are no right answers, only a menu of unappealing choices. Don't expect other people to understand the choices you make.

15. Mania can be quite individual in the way it presents itself. It can, therefore, be confusing when what you're reading or hearing differs a lot from what you're experiencing with your loved one's mania.

16. Keep a journal of changes as they unfold, as well as things you learn. Reread it often so that you stay conscious of what you learn. Also, share this information with the psychiatrist so that changes in medication or other interventions may be considered.

17. A person who is manic can be quite persuasive especially about his belief that there's nothing wrong with him. You may find yourself with dangerous doubts about whether your loved one is sick at all. Remember that this is an illness, one with potentially fatal consequences.

18. A manic person cannot stand to be considered ill when he is feeling on top of the world. He will hammer on your weakest spots to bend you to his way of thinking, namely that he's not sick.

19. If you give in to your doubts, you may be drawn into your person's reality, which can only lead to your feeling more crazy and self-doubting. It is vital to remain shielded as best you can against such feelings. Knowledge and awareness are the best tools, along with professional guidance and support from people who care about you and understand what you're going through.

20. You must be solid within yourself and confident in

Judy Eron

the knowledge that you are dealing with someone who, although seeming in control, although insisting he has total command of himself, is in actuality quite out of control, if not of his present situation, then of the direction his situation is likely to take him. Remember that his judgment is impaired about what is best for him.

This can feel very disloyal, yet is probably the kindest, most responsible attitude you can have. With this attitude, when it becomes necessary, when your loved one plummets, you will be able to assume the responsibility needed. Believing him, trusting that he knows what is best for himself is like trusting a five-year-old to know that playing in the street is dangerous and can get him killed.

21. Mania enhances the confidence of the person who is manic, but may erode the confidence of those who are close to that person because they feel so utterly powerless. You need to guard against this erosion because mania is finite, and when it ends, the even more dangerous phase of depression awaits. You will need all your decision-making skills.

22. During the depressive phase, keep attending (or begin attending) whatever group and individual counseling you have found that deals with manic-depression.

23. Keep your life going. Keep working, keep playing.

24. Spend time with only those friends you feel comfortable with, given what is going on in your life. Dealing with mania is a unique type of stressor. Don't compound your stress by justifying yourself to people who don't understand.

25. Since stress in this situation is inevitable, take care of yourself however you can, even in small ways. Make sure your keys are in your hand before you lock your car door. Check that the burners on your stove are off when you leave home. Make sure you record your checks as you write them. The last thing you need in your life is more chaos.

26. Read as much as you can about this illness and how others have dealt with someone who is manic. Take notes, underline, and refer back to them regularly. *Personal History* by Katherine Graham and *Robert Lowell: A Biography* by Ian Hamilton are two good accounts. (See the bibliography for others.)

27. Without a doubt, you will be abused emotionally. You may decide to bail out if the mania goes on and on, and/or if your loved one refuses to stay on medication and consequently keeps cycling. You are only human. Love is powerful, but in the face of mania, it is not all-powerful.

This is a feeble list when you are looking mania in the face. I know that. I really do know that. But believe me, it is better than no list at all. I know that, too.

I don't want you to lose as I lost. I lost the fight against mania, and I lost the fight against depression. And I lost a beloved partner. That doesn't have to happen—although it may, despite everything you do.

In his book, *Bipolar Disorder Survival Guide*, David J. Miklowitz states:

> It is my strong belief that people who do best with the disorder are those who have learned to recognize triggers and how to minimize the impact of

these triggers. They are people who stay close to their recommended medication regimens and have good relationships with their doctors. They have regular therapists or go to support groups. They have learned as much as they can about the illness, go to conferences where the latest findings about the disorder are presented, talk with others who have the illness, and read books and articles concerning the latest treatments.

This advice also applies to those people who love and are trying to be helpful to the person with manic-depressive illness. Miklowitz goes on to say to the person with the illness:

> Because of the influences of your individual neurophysiology, you should not expect to be able to fully prevent manic episodes. But you have a window of opportunity in the early stages of manic escalation in which you may be able to decrease the severity of your oncoming episode.

He cautions that once a person is in a full-blown manic state, it is too late:

> Mania compares to being in love—giddy, happy, driven, sleepless, more confident, sexual . . . If you were in love, and someone came along with a tablet that would cure you of the feeling, where would you tell that person to go?

Demitri and Janice Papolos in their book, *Overcoming Depression*, put it another way:

> . . . the person experiencing the "highs" of manic-depression often describes feeling better

than at any other time in his life. He cannot understand why anyone would call his experience abnormal or part of an illness.

As I said in my introduction, I do not intend this as a standard how-to book nor as a how-not-to book. It is my wish to merely be there with you in this most unbelievable and disturbing time you are going through, to help balance what you are experiencing. Mania is so far out of our everyday experience, like living in a science-fiction story, that it is too easy to feel quite crazy yourself. I wish to help you to not hate yourself, to not judge yourself, for that will drain you. You need your strength now, and you will need it when your person crashes.

> You tried to fly too fast, and you tried to fly too
>   high.
> But you forgot to take your engines when you
>   went up in the sky,
> And so you landed, not gently,
> On the ground, the very hard ground.
>
> You thought you'd just get up. You thought you'd
>   just brush off.
> You thought you'd prove to everyone that you
>   could stay aloft,
> And we were watching, but we couldn't catch
>   you,
> As you crashed down.

A person who is manic deeply believes that he can and will stay aloft and never crash. But gravity is a fact: What goes up must come down.

I wish you well. I wish you well.

RECOMMENDED RESOURCES

BOOKS

I Am Not Sick, I Don't Need Help! Helping the Seriously Mentally Ill Accept Treatment by Xavier Amador, Ph.D. with Anna-Lisa Johanson. Vida Press, 2000.

My Son, My Son by Iris Bolton with Curtis Mitchell. Bolton Press, 1983.

Bipolar Disorder Demystified: Mastering the Tightrope of Manic-Depression by Lana Castle. Marlowe and Company, 2003.

Loving Someone with Bipolar Disorder by Julie A. Fast and John D. Preston, Psy.D. New Harbinger Publications, 2004.

Surviving Manic Depression: A Manual on Bipoplar

Disorder for Patients, Families, and Providers by E. Fuller Torrey, MD and Michael B. Knable, OD. Basic Books, 2002.

VIDEOS
Coping with Depression by Mary Ellen Copeland.

Understanding and Communicating With a Person Who Is Experiencing Mania by Mary D. Moller, RN. NurSeminars, Inc. 1994.

ORGANIZATIONS & WEBSITES
Depression and Bipolar Support Alliance
(DBSA) 800-826-3632; www.dbsalliance.org

National Alliance for the Mentally Ill
(NAMI) 800-950-NAMI; www.nami.org

Stanley Bipolar Treatment Network
www.bipolarnetwork.org

Bipolar Significant Others (BPSO) www.bpso.org

McMan's Depression and Bipolar Web
www.mcmanweb.com

BIBLIOGRAPHY

Behrman, Andy. *Electroboy: A Memoir of Mania*. Random House, 2002.

Berger, Diane and Lisa. *We Heard the Angels of Madness Singing*. Harper Collins, 1991.

Dowling, Colette. *You Mean I Don't Have to Feel This Way?* Bantam Books, 1993.

Duke, Patty. *A Brilliant Madness*. Bantam Books, 1992.

Fieve, Ronald R., M.D. *Moodswing*. Bantam Books, 1989.

Fine, Carla. *No Time to Say Goodbye*. Doubleday, 1997.

Goodwin, Frederick K. and Kay Redfield Jamison. *Manic-Depressive Illness*. Oxford University Press, 1990.

Graham, Katherine. *Personal History*. Alfred A. Knopf, 1997.

Hamilton, Ian. *Robert Lowell: A Biography*. Random House, 1982.

Bibliography

Hoffman, Jack and Daniel Simon. *Run, Run, Run: The Lives of Abbie Hoffman*. G.P. Putnam Sons, 1994.

Jamison, Kay Redfield. *An Unquiet Mind*. Alfred A. Knopf, 1995.

Jamison, Kay Redfield. *Touched with Fire*. The Free Press, 1993.

Kaplan, Harold I., M.D. and Benjamin J. Sadock, M.D. *Synopsis of Psychiatry*. Williams & Wilkins, 1991.

Keenan, Barbara Mullen. *Every Effort*. St. Martin's Press, 1986.

Kernberg, Otto, et al. *Psychodynamic Psychotherapy of Borderline Patients*. Basic Books, 1989.

Maxmen, Jerrold S. and Nicholas G. Ward. *Essential Psychopathology and Its Treatment*. W.W. Norton, 1995.

Meyers, Jeffrey. *Manic Power: Robert Lowell and His Circle*. Arbor House, 1987.

Miklowitz, David J., Ph.D. *Bipolar Disorder Survival Guide*. Guilford Press, 2002.

Mondimore, Francis Mark, M.D. *Depression: The Mood Disease*. Johns Hopkins University Press, 1993.

Nicholi, Armand M., Jr, ed. *The New Harvard Guide to Psychiatry*. Belknap Press of Harvard University, 1988.

Papolos, Demitri, M.D. and Janice Papolos. *Overcoming Depression*. Harper and Row, 1987.

Styron, William. *Darkness Visible*. Vintage Books, 1990.

DSM IV. American Psychiatric Association, 1994.